OF HOSPITALITY

*Cultural Memory*
*in*
*the*
*Present*

*Mieke Bal and Hent de Vries, Editors*

# OF HOSPITALITY

*Anne Dufourmantelle*
*invites*
*Jacques Derrida*
*to respond*

Translated by
Rachel Bowlby

STANFORD UNIVERSITY PRESS

STANFORD, CALIFORNIA    2000

Stanford University Press
Stanford, California
© 2000 by the Board of Trustees of the
Leland Stanford Junior University

Printed in the United States of America on acid-free, archival-quality paper.

Originally published in French in 1997 under the title *De l'hospitalité: Anne Dufourmantelle invite Jacques Derrida à répondre* by Calmann-Lévy
© 1997 by Calmann-Lévy for the French edition

Assistance for the translation was provided by the French Ministry of Culture.

Library of Congress Cataloging-in-Publication Data

Derrida, Jacques
   [De l'hospitalité. English]
     Of hospitality / Anne Dufourmantelle invites Jacques
Derrida to respond ; translated by Rachel Bowlby.
      p.  cm. — (Cultural memory in the present)
     Includes bibliographical references and index.
     ISBN 0-8047-3405-4 (alk. paper) —
     ISBN 0-8047-3406-2 (paper : alk. paper)
     1. Hospitality.   2. Strangers.   I. Dufourmantelle, Anne.
II. Title.   III. Series.

B2430.D483 D6413 2000
177'.1 — dc21                         00-056359

# Contents

## *Translator's Note*

A pivotal word in these seminars is *étranger*. Like the Greek *xenos*, which figures here as well, the term covers both "stranger" and "foreigner" in English. Because it was more appropriate in most of the contexts, I have used "foreigner" where possible, occasionally substituting "stranger" where necessary or conventional. It seemed necessary when the adjective *étrange* ("strange") was close by, to mark the parallel; and it seemed best to follow convention in mostly translating *xenos* in Greek tragedy as "stranger."

As well as meaning "the stranger" or "the foreigner," *l'étranger* is also equivalent to the English word "abroad." This word is so distant etymologically from either the strange or the foreign that rather than resort to "foreign parts" or some such contrivance when the overlap of person and place was in play, it seemed better simply to lay out the two translations, as in the title to the first seminar. Similarly for the title of the second seminar, where the two meanings of *pas* in "Pas d'hospitalité" cannot be suggested in a single English word, I have given the two translations.

R.B.

OF HOSPITALITY

# Invitation

*Anne Dufourmantelle*

"An act of hospitality can only be poetic."
—Jacques Derrida

*It is Derrida's poetic hospitality that I would like to invoke in these pages, including the difficulty of giving its due to the night—to that which, within a philosophical kind of thinking, does not belong to the order of the day, the visible, and memory. This is to try to come close to a silence around which discourse is ordered, and that a poem sometimes discovers, but always pulls itself back from unveiling in the very movement of speech or writing. If a part of night is inscribed in language, this is also language's moment of effacement.*

*This nocturnal side of speech could be called obsession. A forger can imitate a painter's brush stroke or a writer's style and make the difference between them imperceptible, but he will never be able to make his own their obsession, what forces them to be always going back toward that silence where the first imprints are sealed. Derrida's obsession,[1] in this philosophical narrative woven around that fine theme of hospitality, takes its time in drawing the contours of an impossible, illicit geography of proximity. A proximity that would*

2

# Foreigner Question:

## Coming from Abroad / from the Foreigner

*Question d'étranger: venue de l'étranger*
Fourth seminar (January 10, 1996)

*Jacques Derrida*

Isn't the question of the foreigner [*l'étranger*] a foreigner's question? Coming from the foreigner, from abroad [*l'étranger*]?

Before saying *the* question of the foreigner, perhaps we should also specify: question *of* the foreigner. How should we understand this difference of accent?

There is, we were saying, a question of the foreigner. It is urgent to embark on it—as such.

Of course. But before being a question to be dealt with, before designating a concept, a theme, a problem, a program, the question of the foreigner is a question *of* the foreigner, addressed *to* the foreigner. As though the foreigner were first of all *the one who* puts the first question or *the one to whom* you address the first question. As though the foreigner were being-in-question, the very question of being-in-question, the question-being or being-in-question of the question. But also the one who, putting the first question, puts me in question. One thinks of the

*not be the opposite of an elsewhere come from outside and surrounding it, but "close to the close," that unbearable orb of intimacy that melts into hate. If we can say that murder and hate designate everything that excludes closeness, it is insofar as they ravage from within an original relationship to alterity. The* hostis[2] *responds to hospitality in the way that the ghost recalls himself to the living, not letting them forget. To the pacified reason of Kant, Derrida opposes the primary haunting of a subject prevented by alterity from closing itself off in its peacefulness.*

4

situation of the third person and of justice, which Levinas analyzes as "the birth of the question."

Before reopening this question of the question from the place of the foreigner, and of its Greek situation, as we had said we would, let us limit ourselves to a few remarks or a few readings by way of epigraph.

Back to places we think are familiar: in many of Plato's dialogues, it is often the Foreigner (*xenos*) who questions. He carries and puts the question. We think first of the *Sophist*. It is the Foreigner who, by putting forward the unbearable question, the parricide question, contests the thesis of Parmenides, puts in question the *logos* of our father Parmenides, *ton tou patros Parmenidou logon*. The Foreigner shakes up the threatening dogmatism of the paternal *logos*: the being that is, and the non-being that is not. As though the Foreigner had to begin by contesting the authority of the chief, the father, the master of the family, the "master of the house," of the power of hospitality, of the *hosti-pets* which we have talked about at such length [in earlier seminars].

The Foreigner of the *Sophist* here resembles someone who basically has to account for possibility of sophistry. It is as though the Foreigner were appearing under an aspect that makes you think of a sophist, of someone whom the city or the State is going to treat as a sophist: someone who doesn't speak like the rest, someone who speaks an odd sort of language. But the Xenos asks not to be taken for a parricide. "I will beg one more thing of you," says the Xenos to Theaetetus, "which is not to think of me as a parricide." "What do you mean?"

Theaetetus then asks. The Foreigner: "It is that in order to defend ourselves, we will necessarily have to put to the test the thesis (*logon*) of our father Parmenides and, forcibly, establish that non-being somehow is, and that being, in its turn, in a certain way is not."

This is the fearful question, the revolutionary hypothesis of the Foreigner. He defends himself against the accusation of parricide by denial. He would not dream of defending himself against it if he did not feel deep down that really he is one, a parricide, virtually a parricide, and that to say "non-being is" remains a challenge to Parmenides' paternal logic, a challenge coming from the foreigner. Like any parricide, this one takes place in the family: a foreigner can be a parricide only when he is in some sense within the family. In a minute we will recover some implications of this family scene and this generational difference, indicated by every allusion to the father. Theaetetus's response here is weakened by translation. It registers well the truly polemical, even bellicose character of what is more than a debate ("debate" is the conventional translation for Theaetetus's response) when he says *Phainetai to toiouton diamacheteon en tois logois*: it is obvious, it appears obvious, it certainly seems that that is where one has to fight, *diamacheteon*, engage in a heated combat, *or* that is where one has to carry war into *logoi*, into arguments, into discourses, into the *logos*; and not, as it is peacefully, pacifically put in the Dies translation: "There, obviously, is where we must have the debate" (241d). No, more seriously: "It does seem that that is where there must be armed war, or combat, in discourses or in arguments." The war internal to the *logos*, that is the foreigner's question, the double question, the altercation of father and parricide. It is also the place where the question of the foreigner as a question of hospitality is articulated with the question of being. We know that a reference to the *Sophist* opens [Heidegger's] *Sein und Zeit* as its epigraph.

We ought to reconstitute practically the whole context, if that were possible, and at any rate reread what follows, the sequence that links to the Foreigner's reply. It evokes at once *blindness and madness*, a strange alliance of blindness with madness.

*Blindness* first of all. To Theaetetus's response ("It seems obvious, *phainetai*, that we must have a war around that"), the Foreigner replies in his turn, to raise the stakes: "It is obvious, *even to a blind person*." He says it in the form of a rhetorical question; it is the simulacrum of a question: "How would this not be obvious and, as one says, obvious even to a blind person, *kai to legomenon dè touto tuphlō*?"

Now for *madness*. The Xenos says he is too weak for this kind of combat, for the refutation of the paternal thesis, in view of a possible parricide; he does not have the necessary confidence in himself. How indeed could he have, a parricide Foreigner, so a *foreign son?* Let me insist on the blinding and maddening obviousness: a "foreign *son*," for a parricide can only be a son. In truth, with the question he is getting ready to put, on the being of non-being, the Foreigner fears that he will be treated as mad (*manikos*). He is afraid of being taken for a son-foreigner-madman: "I am therefore fearful that what I have said may give you the opportunity of looking on me as someone deranged," says the translation

9

(literally, mad, *manikos*, a nutter, a maniac), "who is upside down all over (*para poda metaballōn emautōn anō kai katō*), a crazy person who reverses everything from head to toe, from top to bottom, who puts all his feet on his head, inside out, who walks on his head)."

The Foreigner carries and puts the fearful question, he sees or foresees himself, he knows he is already put into question by the paternal and reasonable authority of the *logos*. The paternal authority of the *logos* gets ready to disarm him, to treat him as mad, and this at the very moment when his question, the question *of* the Foreigner, only seems to contest in order then to remind people of what ought to be obvious even to the blind!

That the Foreigner here figures, virtually, a parricide son, both blind and super-seeing, seeing in the blind place of the blind person—here is something that is not foreign to a certain Oedipus we will see crossing the border in a moment. For it will be a question of the arrival of Oedipus, this will be *the* question, from the arrival of this blind Foreigner leaning on Antigone—who sees for him. It is Oedipus, upon his arrival in the city, whom we will summon to appear when the time comes.

In the meantime, to stay a little bit longer with Plato, we could also have reread the *Statesman*. There again a Foreigner takes the initiative with the fearful, even intolerable question. The Foreigner is moreover warmly welcomed, apparently, he is given asylum, he has the right to hospitality; Socrates' first words, from the first sentence of the dialogue, are to thank Theodorus for having introduced him to Theaetetus, certainly, but also, at the same time, the

*ship that gives this thinking its uniqueness, its partic-
ular genius.*

*Derrida has himself spoken of the difficulty of tak-
ing account of the open speech of the seminar as it relates to hospitality. "What I don't want to say or cannot, the unsaid, the forbidden, what is passed over in
silence, what is separated off . . . —all these should be
interpreted," he stressed. "In these regions we rediscover
the open question of the relationship between hospitality and the question, in other words of a hospitality beginning with the name, the question of the name, or*

Foreigner ("*hama kai tes tou xenou*"). And the question that the Foreigner will address to them to open this great debate, which will also be a great combat, is nothing less than the question of the statesman, of man as a political being. Better, the question of the political person, of the statesman, *after* the question of the sophist. For the dialogue the *Statesman* (*Politicos*) would come, in time and in logic, in the chrono-logic of Plato's oeuvre and discourse, after the *Sophist*. Now the Foreigner's leading question in the *Statesman*, after the question of the sophist, is just that—the question of the statesman. The Xenos says (258b): "Well then, after the sophist, it's the statesman (the political man, *ton politikon andra*) that we are going to have to seek out (*diazètein*). So tell me, should we classify him among those who know (*tōn epistemonōn*)?" Yes, replies the young Socrates, the other Socrates. The Foreigner concludes from this that it is therefore necessary to begin by distinguishing between forms of knowledge as we were doing, he says, when we studied the previous character, in other words the sophist.

Sometimes the foreigner is Socrates himself, Socrates the disturbing man of question and irony (which is to say, of question, another meaning of the word "irony"), the man of the midwifely question. Socrates himself has the characteristics of the foreigner, he represents, he figures the foreigner, he *plays* the foreigner he is not. In particular he does it in what is for us an extremely interesting scene—of which Henri Joly reminds us at the start of the fine posthumous book I recommended you read: *La question des étrangers* [*The Question of Foreigners*] (Paris: Vrin, 1992).

13

*else opening up without question. . . . " And also: "One could dream about what would be the lesson of some- one who didn't have the keys to his own knowledge, who didn't arrogate it to himself. He would give place to the place, leaving the keys with the other to unlock the words from their enclosure."*

It is this *"giving place to the place"* that, I think, is the promise kept by these words. They also make us un- derstand the question of place as being a fundamental question, founding the history of our culture and un- thought in it. It would be consenting to exile, in other

In *The Apology of Socrates* (17d), at the very beginning of his defense, Socrates addresses his fellow citizens and Athenian judges. He defends himself against the accusation of being a kind of sophist or skillful speaker. He announces that he is going to say what is right and true, certainly, against the liars who are accusing him, but without rhetorical elegance, without flowery use of language. He declares that he is "foreign" to the language of the courts, to the tribune of the tribunals: he doesn't know how to speak this courtroom language, this legal rhetoric of accusation, defense, and pleading; he doesn't have the skill, he is *like* a foreigner. (Among the serious problems we are dealing with here is that of the foreigner who, inept at speaking the language, always risks being without defense before the law of the country that welcomes or expels him; the foreigner is first of all foreign to the legal language in which the duty of hospitality is formulated, the right to asylum, its limits, norms, policing, etc. He has to ask for hospitality in a language which by definition is not his own, the one imposed on him by the master of the house, the host, the king, the lord, the authorities, the nation, the State, the father, etc. This personage imposes on him translation into their own language, and that's the first act of violence. That is where the question of hospitality begins: must we ask the foreigner to understand us, to speak our language, in all the senses of this term, in all its possible extensions, before being able and so as to be able to welcome him into our country? If he was already speaking our language, with all that that implies, if we already shared everything that is shared with a language, would the foreigner still be a for-

15

eigner and could we speak of asylum or hospitality in regard to him? This is the paradox that we are going to see become clearer.)

What does Socrates say at the moment when, let's not forget it, he is playing for his life and is soon going to lose it in this game? What does he say in presenting himself as *like* a foreigner, at once *as though* he were a foreigner (as a fiction) and *inasmuch as* in effect he does become the foreigner by language (a condition that he is even going to lay claim to, whatever he says about it, by a skillful courtroom denial), a foreigner accused in a language he says he doesn't speak, a defendant required to justify himself, in the language of the other, before the law and the judges of the city? He thus addresses his fellow citizens, the Athenian judges, whom he sometimes calls "Athenians." They speak as (or like) judges, the citizens who speak in the name of their citizenship. Socrates turns the situation on its head: he asks them to treat him like a foreigner for whom marks of respect can be demanded, a foreigner because of his age and a foreigner because of his language, the only language he is used to; it is either that of philosophy, or everyday language, popular language (as opposed to the clever language of the judges or of sophistry, of rhetoric and juridical jargon):

No, what you will hear will be a straightforward speech in the first words that occur to me, confident as I am of the justice of my cause, and I do not want any of you to expect anything different. It would hardly be suitable, gentlemen, for a man of my age to address you in the artificial language of a schoolboy orator. One thing, however, I do most earnestly beg and entreat of you. If you

Movements of speaking

*It is difficult to hear something of the rightness of a way of speaking without taking the measure of its step, which is to say its rhythm, and the time necessary to say it. "The how of truth is precisely truth," wrote Kierkegaard.[3] I will thus concentrate on listening to the particular "how" of Derrida's thinking, rather than on the sterile exercize of commentary. "The philosopher needs a double hearing," insisted Nietzsche, "in the way* hear me defending myself in the same language which it has been my habit to use, both in the market square next to the stalls—where many of you have heard me—and elsewhere, do not be surprised, and do not interrupt. Let me remind you of my position. This is my first appearance in a court of law, at the age of seventy, and so I am a complete foreigner to the language of this place [a complete foreigner is *atechnōs oun xenos echo tes enthade lexeos*: *atechnōs*, with an omega, means "simply, completely, absolutely," and this is why it is correct to translate it as "a complete foreigner"; but that means "simply, absolutely, completely" because it means first of all "simply, without artifice, without *techne*, very close to *atechnos*, with a short *o*, which does mean, precisely, inexperienced, without technique, inept, without savoir-faire: I am simply foreign, purely and simply a foreigner with no aptitude, without recourse or resources]. Now if I were really a foreigner [*ei tō onti xenos etugkanon ōn*], you would naturally excuse me if I spoke in the accent and dialect in which I had been brought up [the accent is *phōnè*; the dialect or idiolect is *tropos*, the trope, the turning, the turns of rhetoric that suit an idiom; in short, ways of speaking].[1]

This passage teaches us something else. Joly reminds us of it, as does Benveniste, whom I'll be quoting in a moment: at Athens, the foreigner had some rights. He saw he had a recognized right of access to the courts, since Socrates assumes it: if I were a foreigner, here in the court, he says, you would tolerate not only my accent, my voice, my elocution, but the turns of phrase in my spontaneous, original, idiomatic rhetoric. There is thus a foreigners' right, a right of hospitality for foreigners at Athens. What is the subtlety of Socratic rhetoric, of Socrates the Athenian's plea? It consists of complaining at not even being treated as a foreigner: if

I were foreign, you would accept with more toler-
ance that I don't speak as you do, that I have my
own idiom, my way of speaking that is so far from
being technical, so far from juridical, a way that is
at once more popular and more philosophical. That
the foreigner, the *xenos*, is not simply the absolute
other, the barbarian, the savage absolutely excluded
and heterogeneous—this is Benveniste's point as
well, same article as before, when he starts on Greek
institutions, after the generalities and the paradoxical filiation of *hostis*, which we have said a lot about
in the last few seminars. Following the logic of this
argument we were discussing last time on the subject of the reciprocity and equality of "for" in ex-
change (I won't go back over it). Benveniste em-
phasizes that "the same institution exists in the
Greek world under another name: *xenos* indicates
relations of the same type between men linked by a
pact which implies precise obligations also extend-
ing to their descendants."[2]

    This last point—we take its measure right away—
is critical. This pact, this contract of hospitality that
links *to* the foreigner and which *reciprocally* links
the foreigner, it's a question of knowing whether it
counts beyond the individual and if it also extends
to the family, to the generation, to the genealogy. It
is not, here, although the things are connected, a
question of the classical problem of the right to nationality or citizenship as a *birth*right—in some
places linked to the land and in others to blood. It
is not only a question of the link between birth and
nationality; it is not only a question of the citizenship offered to someone who had none previously,
but of the right granted to the foreigner as such, to

the foreigner remaining a foreigner, and to his or her relatives, to the family, to the descendants.

This familial or genealogical right applying to more than one generation enables us to think about how this is not, basically, a question of the extension of the right or the "pact" (to use Benveniste's term; he wants to insist on the reciprocity of the commitment: the foreigner doesn't only have a right, he or she also has, reciprocally, obligations, as is often recalled, whenever there is a wish to reproach him for bad behavior); it is not a question of a straightforward extension of an individual right, of opening out to the family and subsequent generations a right in the first place granted to the individual. No, that reflects, that lets us reflect upon the fact that, from the outset, the right to hospitality commits a household, a line of descent, a family, a familial or ethnic group receiving a familial or ethnic group. Precisely because it is inscribed in a right, a custom, an *ethos* and a *Sittlichkeit*, this objective morality that we were speaking about last time presupposes the social and familial status of the contracting parties, that it is possible for them to be called by their names, to have names, to be subjects in law, to be questioned and liable, to have crimes imputed to them, to be held responsible, to be equipped with nameable identities, and proper names. A proper name is never purely individual.

If we wanted to pause for a moment on this significant fact, we would have to note once again a paradox or a contradiction: this right to hospitality offered to a foreigner "as a family," represented and protected by his or her family name, is at once what makes hospitality possible, or the hospitable rela-

room for astonishment, for what breaks reflection in the seizure of fear.

Why fear? The word seems too violent just to say "what astonishes." And yet that is certainly what it's about, not a fear produced by the devastating or dominating effect of the speech itself, but that space of the unknowable that the speech apprehends and before which it stops us short for a moment, scared. Just as, in a musical score, the markings for silences make the melodic line enter into dialogue with the silence that sustains it, so philosophical speech espouses the precise

tionship to the foreigner possible, but by the same token what limits and prohibits it. Because hospitality, in this situation, is not offered to an anonymous new arrival and someone who has neither name, nor patronym, nor family, nor social status, and who is therefore treated not as a foreigner but as another barbarian. We have alluded to this: the difference, one of the subtle and sometimes ungraspable differences between the foreigner and the absolute other is that the latter cannot have a name or a family name; the absolute or unconditional hospitality I would like to offer him or her presupposes a break with hospitality in the ordinary sense, with conditional hospitality, with the right to or pact of hospitality. In saying this, once more, we are taking account of an irreducible pervertibility. The law of hospitality, the express law that governs the general concept of hospitality, appears as a paradoxical law, pervertible or perverting. It seems to dictate that absolute hospitality should break with the law of hospitality as right or duty, with the "pact" of hospitality. To put it in different terms, absolute hospitality requires that I open up my home and that I give not only to the foreigner (provided with a family name, with the social status of being a foreigner, etc.), but to the absolute, unknown, anonymous other, and that I *give place* to them, that I let them come, that I let them arrive, and take place in the place I offer them, without asking of them either reciprocity (entering into a pact) or even their names. The law of absolute hospitality commands a break with hospitality by right, with law or justice as rights. Just hospitality breaks with hospitality by right; not that it condemns or is opposed to it, and it can on the contrary set and maintain it in a perpetual progressive movement; but it is as strangely heterogeneous to it as justice is heterogeneous to the law to which it is yet so close, from which in truth it is indissociable.

Now the foreigner, the *xenos* of whom Socrates says "him at least you would respect, you would tolerate his accent and his idiom," or the one of whom Benveniste says that he enters into a pact, this foreigner who has the right to hospitality in the cosmopolitan tradition which will find its most powerful form in Kant and the text we have read and reread [*Perpetual Peace*], this foreigner, then, is someone with whom, to receive him, you begin by asking his name; you enjoin him to state and to guarantee his identity, as you would a witness before a court. This is someone to whom you put a question and address a demand, the first demand, the minimal demand being: "What is your name?" or then "In telling me what your name is, in responding to this request, you are responding on your own behalf, you are responsible before the law and before your hosts, you are a subject in law."

That, following one of the directions it takes, is the question of the foreigner as the question of the question. Does hospitality consist in interrogating the new arrival? Does it begin with the question addressed to the newcomer (which seems very human and sometimes loving, assuming that hospitality should be linked to love—an enigma that we will leave in reserve for the moment): what is your name? tell me your name, what should I call you, I who am calling on you, I who want to call you by your name? What am I going to call you? It is also what we sometimes tenderly ask children and those we love. Or else does hospitality begin with the un-questioning welcome, in a double effacement, the effacement of the question *and* the name? Is it more just and more loving to question or not to question? to call by the name or without the name? to give or to learn a name already given? Does one give hospi-tality to a subject? to an identifiable subject? to a subject identifiable by name? to a legal subject? Or is hospitality *rendered*, is it *given* to the other before they are identified, even before they are (posited as or supposed to be) a subject, legal subject and sub-ject nameable by their family name, etc.?

The question of hospitality is thus also the ques-tion of the question; but by the same token the question of the subject and the name as hypothesis of descent.

When Benveniste wants to define the *xenos*, there is nothing fortuitous in his beginning from the *xenia*. He inscribes the *xenos* in the *xenia*, which is to say in the pact, in the contract or collective alliance of that name. Basically, there is no *xenos*, there is no foreigner before or outside the *xenia*, this pact or ex-change with a group or, to be more precise, with a line of descent. Herodotus said that Polycrates had concluded a *xenia* (pact) with Amasis and that they sent each other presents: *xenien sunethèkato* (verb for pact: they concluded, like a pact, a *xenia*) *pem-pōn dōra kai dechomenos alla par'ekeivou*, in sending and receiving gifts, reciprocally, from each other. If we reread Benveniste we would find other examples of the same type. To have done with this epigraph, let us just recall a Socratic commonplace. He too oc-cupies, elsewhere, that position of foreigner, and indeed in a strange scene of the question, of the inverted question-response, if I can put it like that. Far from himself interrogating or appealing to the law and rights of the city, he is himself questioned, apostrophized by the Laws. They address themselves to him to ask him questions, but false questions, simulated questions, "rhetorical questions." Trick questions. All he can reply is what the Laws, in their prosopopeia, wish and expect him to reply. It is the famous Prosopopeia of the Laws in the *Crito*, which you should read closely for yourselves; I am just going to give a sense of the attack, as it were. Socrates is still, this time after being condemned to death, pretending to behave as a foreigner, ready to leave the city without authorization, to escape Athens by challenging the Laws of the city. These then speak to him to put those catch questions, those impossible questions.

At the start of this passage is the entrance of the Laws, *hoi nomoi*. Entrance staged by Socrates, by Plato's Socrates who thus speaks across the face of the Laws, across the voice of their prosopopeia. Prosopopeia, in other words, the face, the mask, and first of all the voice that speaks across this mask, a *persona*, a voice without a look (in a moment this will be the blind man's portrait and the voice of Oedipus, the foreigner addressing foreigners at the moment when, leaning on Antigone, he arrives in Colonus):

SOCRATES: Look at it like this. Suppose that while we were preparing to run away from here—or however one should describe it—the laws and state of Athens were to come and confront us and ask this question: "Now, Socrates, what are you proposing to do? Can you deny

*"the other" (the guest), and moves on to examine an-*
*other question. Yet sometimes, and Levinas has spoken*
*so well about this, it lets itself lose its bearings.*

*One of the names for this being at a loss, in philos-*
*ophy, is astonishment. But astonishment turns us to-*
*ward that moment when fear yields to being set on the*
*path of familiarity, discovering other fords along the*
*way, other marks to become accustomed to.*

*Astonishment is the precise name for what Derrida's*
*speaking calls forth in us. It forces us finally to think,*
*and no longer to imagine that we are thinking. I add*

that by this act which you are contemplating you intend, so far as you have the power, to destroy us, the laws, and the whole state as well? Do you think that a state can exist and not be turned upside down, if the legal judgments which are pronounced in it have no force but are nullified and destroyed by private persons?" How shall we answer this question, Crito, and others like it? There is much that could be said, especially by a professional advocate, to protest against the invalidation of this law which enacts that judgments once pronounced shall be binding. Shall we say, "Yes, I do intend to destroy the laws, because the state wronged me by passing an incorrect judgment at my trial?" Is this to be our answer, or what?

CRITO: Definitely, Socrates.

SOCRATES: But what if the Laws say: "Socrates, is that what was agreed between us and you, or was it to abide by whatever judgments the state made?"

And if we expressed surprise at such language, they would probably say, "Never mind our language, Socrates, but answer our questions; after all, you are used to the question and answer approach. Now then, what charge are you bringing against us and the state, to be trying to destroy us? Did we not give you life in the first place? Was it not through us that your father married your mother and became your parent? Tell us, is there something you find wrong with those of us laws that deal with marriages?"

"No, there isn't," I would say.

"Well, is there anything you find wrong with the laws that deal with children's upbringing and education, such as you had yourself? Or haven't they been right in their orders, those of us laws which were instituted for this end, for requiring your father to give you a cultural and physical education?"[3]

So Socrates appears in the guise of a foreigner on the outskirts of Athens. He thinks of escaping once he

*that it also takes the risk of the other in the play of the seminar. It accepts the risk of being wrongly understood, wrongly interpreted, sanctified, demonized, or else interrupted point-blank, and thus the risk that the discourse can be driven off its course, to inaugurate a dialogue where nothing was planned. I would like to*

has been condemned to death but gives up the idea of leaving the city when the Laws address him to interrogate him, really to put false questions to him. With this figure of the foreigner—both to liken them by analogy and to distinguish them, if not to contrast them—we could compare the figure of Oedipus, the outlaw (*anomon*). Not at the moment of departure, the moment when he separates off, leaves or pretends to leave the city, like Socrates, but at the moment when he enters Colonus. We will probably come back to this story at some length; but still by way of epigraph and to leave things in suspense, here are two moments where Oedipus the foreigner, the *xenos*, addresses the inhabitants of this country like foreigners. The foreigner speaks to foreigners, that is what he calls them. The first moment, then, is the arrival of the arrival, Oedipus. A foreigner prepares to speak to the foreigner. Without knowledge. Without the knowledge, the knowledge of the place, and the knowledge of the name of the place: where he is, where he is going. Between the profane and the sacred, the human or the divine. Isn't this always the situation of the absolute arrival? Foreigner's request to foreigner:

OEDIPUS: Child of a blind old man, Antigone—where have we come to now? Whose city is this? Who today will receive the wandering Oedipus with a little hospitality? . . . But if, my child, you see a place to sit, whether on ordinary or sacred ground, stop me and set me down there, so that we can find out where we are. We have come here as foreigners to learn from the natives and do what they say. . . .

Sit me down there, then, and look after the blind man. . . .

*salute the audacity that leads a philosophical utterance to make us desert those dwellings of the mind where reason lives as master, when for an instant astonishment makes reason a guest.*

Scanning of thought around the night which holds it. Figures of obsession.

*What is this "night" from whose depths a philosophical utterance is outlined? In his very fine book*

ANTIGONE: Shall I go now and ask what place it is?

OEDIPUS: Yes, child, as long as it is habitable.

ANTIGONE: It is even inhabited. But I think there is no need. I can see a man right here close to us. . . . So say what you think is a good idea, for here he is.

OEDIPUS: Stranger, hearing from this girl who sees for both of us that you have luckily turned up as a messenger to tell us what we are unclear about. . . .

STRANGER: Before you ask me anything else, get up from that seat. You are on land that is not meant for walking on.

OEDIPUS: What land is it? Is it dedicated to one of the gods, then?

STRANGER: It must not be sat on or dwelt on. It belongs to the goddesses of fear, the daughters of Earth and Darkness.[4]

These are the Eumenides, "who see everything, so the local people will tell you." It will not be long before Oedipus invokes the "respite" promised by Phoebus from all his misfortunes, at the time when, "in a last country," he would find himself offered "shelter and hospitality" from the fearful goddesses. This foreign guest appears like a ghost. He asks pity for the "worthless phantom of the one who was Oedipus." And when the chorus calls him a "wanderer" who is "not a native," Oedipus begs that, even though he is a phantom, he not be taken for an "outlaw" (*anomon*).[5]

The second moment we would choose to select by way of epigraph would be the moment of the chorus. At that point it is not the Laws who speak,

The Heretical Essays, *published secretly in Prague, Jan Patočka put night, which should here be understood as an ontological figure, in opposition to the values of the day. "Man is meant to let grow in him what provokes anxiety, what is unreconciled, what is enigmatic, what ordinary life turns away from so as to get to the present agenda."[6] Patočka interpreted the crisis of the modern world and the decline of Europe in terms of a totalitarianism of everyday knowledge. To reason on the basis of the values of the day is to be prompted by the wish to define and subjugate the real solely in order to attain a*

as they do when they address Socrates. The chorus apostrophizes Oedipus. It addresses the foreigner who bears a terrible secret. What he knows threatens to place him outside the law, situates him outside the law in advance: Oedipus who has committed incest and parricide, a well-known scene that we should have to read from another angle. What angle? What is an angle, here, in what is no longer simply a triangle? The angle from which you perceive this, a strange accusation, a counter-accusation, an indictment? To vindicate himself, in a way to plead his case, Oedipus does accuse, he accuses without accusing anyone, he accuses something rather than someone. In fact he denounces the figure of a city, Thebes. The guilty one is Thebes. It is Thebes which, without knowing it, unconcious Thebes, the city-unconscious, the unconscious at the heart of the town, the *polis*, the political unconscious (this is why the accusation incriminates without incriminating: how could you put on trial an unconscious or a city, where neither of the two could answer for their acts?)—it is Thebes, then, which, unawares, bears the responsibility for the crime. The unconscious (of) Thebes would be rendered *unforgivably* guilty of Oedipus's incest, parricide, and being-outside-the-law.

How can the unforgivable be forgiven? But what else can be forgiven?

It is the law of the city that, without wishing or knowing it, drove him to crime, to incest and parricide: this law must have produced the outside-the-law. There is nothing surprising in that, ultimately. This scene of parricide is regularly to be found wherever there is a question of foreignness and hospital-

quantifiable knowledge pledged to technological values. If we separate darkness from clarity, we will suffer its ravages, Patočka predicted; what we should rather be doing is taking our attention right up to the edge of this darkness. Interpreting clarity in terms of its belonging to night as well is also, I think, one of the paths that Derrida's reflections have opened up.

Since those wanderers called Oedipus and Antigone make an appearance in the course of the seminar, I would like to return for a moment to Patočka's reading of Antigone.[7]

ity, as soon as the host, the one receiving, also commands. According to the chain we are now familiar with (*hosti-pet-s*, *potis*, *potest*, *ipse*, etc.), the sovereignty of power, the host's *potestas* and possession, remain those of the *paterfamilias*, the head of the house, the *maître de céans*, as Klossowski calls him. And the same word is translated in two ways, sometimes by *étranger* [stranger or foreigner], sometimes by *hôte* [host]. That is understandable, no doubt. It reminds us of or intimates the necessity of a passage, in culture, between the two meanings of the word *xenos*, but strictly speaking it remains hard to justify.

CHORUS: It is dreadful, stranger, to reawaken a bad thing long laid to rest. All the same I am longing to know. . . .

OEDIPUS: What is this?

CHORUS: . . . about that awful pain, irresistibly appearing, that you became embroiled in.

OEDIPUS: In the name of your hospitality (*xenias*), don't ruthlessly open up what I suffered.

CHORUS: There is a widespread and constant rumor, and I ask, stranger (*xein'*), to hear it truly told. . . .

OEDIPUS: I suffered the worst things, strangers, I endured them even willingly, let the gods be witness. But none of these things were my own choice. . . . By a sinful union the city bound me, in my ignorance, to the ruins caused by my marriage.

CHORUS: Did you really, as I have heard, go into a marriage bed that got a bad name from your mother?

OEDIPUS: Oh! It is death to me to hear that, stranger. These two girls of mine . . . these two children, two misfortunes . . . were born like me from the same mother's labor.

*The mythical character in Sophocles'* Antigone *captivates us because she keeps herself close to the origins. "She is one of those who love, not one of those who hate," wrote Patočka, but this love is not Christlike. It signifies "love as foreign to the human condition, deriving from the portion of night which is the portion of the gods."*[8] *In the confrontation between Creon and Antigone, Patočka shows that the force of law represented by Creon is really a response to fear, for it is "on fear that the sphere of day depends, the State as he conceives it." This fear under its final mask is the fear of*

CHORUS: So they are both your offspring. . . .

OEDIPUS: And also their father's sisters. . . .

CHORUS: You did. . . .

OEDIPUS: I did not do. . . . I received a gift from the city when I had done it a favor that, miserable one, I should never have accepted.

CHORUS: And then, unhappy one? You murdered. . . .

OEDIPUS: What are you saying? What do you want to know?

CHORUS: . . . your father? . . . You killed.

OEDIPUS: I did kill, but . . . there is some justice on my side. . . . I was driven mad by a destructive power when I murdered and destroyed, but in law I am innocent. It was in ignorance that I came to this.[6]

When he arrives, Theseus takes pity on the blind man. He has not forgotten, he says, that he too "grew up as a foreigner" (562) and put his life at risk "in a foreign land" (563). Like the oath to come, the exchange makes an alliance between two foreigners.

After this long epigraph, let us begin again. Although it is intimately associated with, and although it remains familiarly linked to, the notion of the *hostis* as host or as enemy (an ambivalence that we have been meditating or premeditating at length up to this point), we had not yet broached the strange notion of "foreigner" for itself.

What does "foreigner" mean? Who is foreign? Who is the foreign man, who is the foreign woman? What is meant by "going abroad," "coming from abroad"? We had merely stressed that, if at least we have to give it a determinate scope, a normal usage,

*death. "Thus Creon himself testifies, without realizing it, to his dependence in relation to the other, in relation to the law of Night. And as Antigone embodies the law, the portion of night, it is pointless to threaten her with death."*[9] *Here Patočka is writing against what has associated our consciousness with the monopolizing of a meaning it thought it could make use of. "Sophocles'* Antigone *represents the reminder of a tiny hope, a reminder that Creon's way of thinking has completely hidden in us: the fact that man does not belong to himself, that his meaning is not Meaning, that*

as it is used most often, *sensu stricto*, when the context does not specify it more (the normal meaning is almost always the most "narrow" meaning, obviously), *étranger* is understood on the basis of the cirmcumscribed field of *ethos* or ethics, of habitat or time spent as *ethos*, of *Sittlichkeit*, of objective morality, especially in the three instances determined by law and Hegel's philosophy of law: the *family*, *bourgeois* or *civil society*, and the *State* (or the nation-state). We had elaborated and interrogated these limits at length, and we asked ourselves a certain number of questions—stemming from but also on the subject of interpretations of Benveniste, especially based on the two Latin derivations: the foreigner (*hostis*) welcomed as guest or as enemy. Hospitality, hostility, *hostpitality*. As always, the Benveniste readings had seemed to us as valuable as they were problematic—let's not go back to that here.

Today, and on that basis, let us broach more directly the meaning of *étranger*, this time from the "Greek world" (to presuppose provisionally its unity or self-identity), but always by doing our best, since it isn't an easy thing, to multiply the two-way journeys, a to-and-fro between the matters of urgency that assail us at this end-of-millennium, and the tradition from which we receive the concepts, the vocabulary, the axioms that are elementary and presumed natural or untouchable. It is often techno-political-scientific mutation that obliges us to deconstruct; really, such mutation itself deconstructs what are claimed as these naturally obvious things or these untouchable axioms. For instance, from the Latin or Greek tradition that we have just mentioned.

45

So we were trying, the other day, to translate into our hospitality problematic what it is that turns up, what comes our way by e-mail or the Internet. Among the innumerable signs of mutation that accompany the development of e-mail and the Internet—I mean everything that these names stand for—let us first privilege those that completely transform the structure of so-called public space. We have just been speaking about the *xenos* and *xenia* in Greece, and about Oedipus and Antigone as *xenoi* addressing *xenoi* who speak to them, in return, reciprocally, as *xenoi*—and we'll be doing so again, later. But how could Sophocles' semantics, for example, have held up in a public space structured by the telephone, the fax, e-mail, and the Internet, by all those other prosthetic apparatuses of television and telephonic blindness? What we were wondering the other day was what the intervention of a State (it happened the other day in Germany) or a State chorus seeking to ban or censure so-called "pornographic" communications on an Internet site can mean nowadays. Not Klossowski's *Lois de l'hospitalité* [*Laws of Hospitality*], but some texts and images distributed on the Internet. The German government banned two hundred pornographic sites (*Le canard enchaîné* points out in this connection that some censors who detected the pornographic connotations of the word "breast" blocked access to a forum where patients with breast cancer were innocently in dialogue). Let me not take sides right now on the validity of these forms of censorship and their principles, but rather analyze, as a beginning, the facts of a problem. Nowadays, a reflection on hospitality presupposes, among other things, the possibility of a rigorous delimitation of

47

thresholds or frontiers: between the familial and the non-familial, between the foreign and the non-foreign, the citizen and the non-citizen, but first of all between the private and the public, private and public law, etc. In principle, private mail in the classic form (the letter, the postcard, etc.) has to circulate without control within a country or from one country to another. It must be neither read nor intercepted. The same is true, in principle, for the phone, the fax, e-mail, and naturally for the Internet. Censorship, telephone tapping, interceptions, in principle represent either crimes or acts authorized only for reasons of State, of a State responsible for the integrity of the territory, for sovereignty, for security and national defense. So what happens when a State intervenes not only for surveillance but to ban private communications, on the pretext that they are pornographic, which, up to now, hasn't been a danger to public security or the integrity of national territory? I assume, without knowing enough about it, that the argument by which this state intervention claims to be justified is the allegation that the space of the Internet is in fact not private but public, and above all has a public accessibility (nationally or internationally) greatly exceeding, in its usage, in its resources, that of "porn" links by phone or video network. And even more greatly exceeding the readership of Sade, of *Lois de l'hospitalité* and other similar works that are in a way self-censoring, because their number of readers is automatically reduced by the "competence" they require. At any rate, what is at issue, and is by the same token "deranged," deformed, is once again the trace of a frontier between the public and the non-public, between public or political space and individual or familial home. The frontier turns out to be caught in a juridico-political turbulence, in the process of destructuration-restructuration, challenging existing law and established norms. From the moment when a public authority, a State, this or that State power, gives itself or is recognized as having the right to control, monitor, ban exchanges that those doing the exchanging deem private, but that the State can intercept since these private exchanges cross public space and become available there, then every element of hospitality gets disrupted. My "at home" was also constituted by the field of access via my telephone line (through which I can give my time, my word, my friendship, my love, my help, to whomever I wish, and so invite whomever I wish to come into my home, first in my ear, when I wish, at any time of the day or night, whether the other is my across-the-fence neighbor, a fellow citizen, or any other friend or person I don't know at the other end of the world). Now if my "home," in principle inviolable, is also constituted, and in a more and more essential, interior way, by my phone line, but also by my e-mail, but also by my fax, but also by my access to the Internet, then the intervention of the State becomes a violation of the inviolable, in the place where inviolable immunity remains the condition of hospitality.

The possibilities we are thus invoking are not more abstract or improbable than phone tapping. These phone tappings are practiced not only by police forces or State security services. In Germany, a few weeks ago, I was reading a news item in a daily paper about some appliances for sale on the open

selves under a permanently dual law. What Derrida gets us to understand is that the opposite of nearness is not elsewhere but another figure of nearness. And I think this geography leads throughout the seminar to the revelation of the question "Where?" as being the question of man. A question which, like that of the Sphinx, is addressed to a man on the move, who has no other place of his own than that of being on the way, bound for a destination that is unknown to him, but precedes him with its shadow.

The question "Where?" is ageless, transitive, it gives

market (some 20,000 of them had already been sold when the German law started to get worried). These appliances would make it possible not just to eavesdrop on any phone conversation across a wide perimeter (500 meters in circumference, I believe), but even to record them, which opens up unprecedented options for private spying and blackmail. All these techno-scientific possibilities threaten the interiority of the home ("we are no longer at home!") and really the very integrity of the self, of ipseity. These possibilities are experienced as threats bearing down on the particular territory of one's own and on the law of private property. They are obviously behind all the purifying reactions and feelings of resentment. Wherever the "home" is violated, wherever at any rate a violation is felt as such, you can foresee a privatizing and even familialist reaction, by widening the ethnocentric and nationalist, and thus xenophobic, circle: not directed against the foreigner as such, but, paradoxically, against the anonymous technological power (foreign to the language or the religion, as much as to the family and the nation), which threatens, with the "home," the traditional conditions of hospitality. The perversion and pervertibility of this law (which is also a law of hospitality) is that one can become virtually xenophobic in order to protect or claim to protect one's own hospitality, the own home that makes possible one's own hospitality. (Remember as well the xenotransplantation we were talking about last time.) I want to be master at home (*ipse*, *potis*, *potens*, head of house, we have seen all that), to be able to receive whomever I like there. Anyone who encroaches on my "at home," on my ipseity, on my power of hospitality, on my sovereignty as host, I start to regard as an undesirable foreigner, and virtually as an enemy. This other becomes a hostile subject, and I risk becoming their hostage.

Paradoxical and corrupting law: it depends on this constant collusion between traditional hospitality, hospitality in the ordinary sense, and power. This collusion is also power in its *finitude*, which is to say the necessity, for the host, for the one who receives, of choosing, electing, filtering, selecting their invitees, visitors, or guests, those to whom they decide to grant asylum, the right of visiting, or hospitality. No hospitality, in the classic sense, without sovereignty of oneself over one's home, but since there is also no hospitality without finitude, sovereignty can only be exercised by filtering, choosing, and thus by excluding and doing violence. Injustice, a certain injustice, and even a certain perjury, begins right away, from the very threshold of the right to hospitality. This collusion between the violence of power or the force of law (*Gewalt*) on one side, and hospitality on the other, seems to depend, in an absolutely radical way, on hospitality being inscribed in the form of a right, this kind of inscription we have said a lot about in the course of previous seminars. But since this right, whether private or familial, can only be exercised and guaranteed by the mediation of a public right or State right, the perversion is unleashed from the inside. For the State cannot guarantee or claim to guarantee the private domain (for it is a domain), other than by controlling it and trying to penetrate it to be sure of it. Of course, in controlling it, which can appear negative and repressive, it can claim, by the same token, to protect it, to enable communication, to extend information and openness. The painful paradox stems from this coextensiveness between the democratization of information and the scope of the police and politics: as the powers of the police and politicization are extended, so communication, permeability, and democratic openness extend their space and their phenomenality, their appearing in broad daylight.

The blessing of visibility and daylight is *also* what the police and politics demand. Even the so-called secret police and politics, a particular police and a particular politics that often, and with good reason, present themselves as being the police and politics in their entirety. This was always the case, but today the accelerated deployment of particular technologies increases more rapidly than ever the scope and power of what is called private sociality, far beyond the territory of measurable-surveyable space, where it has never been possible to keep it anyway. So today, through the phone, the fax, e-mail, and the Internet, etc., this private sociality is tending to extend its antennae beyond national-state territory at the speed of light. Therefore the State, suddenly smaller, weaker than these non-State private powers, both infra- and supra-state—the classical State, or the cooperation of classical States—makes excessive efforts to catch and monitor, contain and reappropriate to itself the very thing that is escaping it as fast as possible. This sometimes takes the form of a rearrangement of the law, of new legal texts, but also of new police ambitions attempting to adapt to the new powers of communication and information, in other words also to new spaces of hospitality.

Phone tapping remains almost impossible to control; it is increasing every day even if, technologically, it cuts a somewhat archaic figure. Nowadays it is e-mail that is monitored. Recently, in New York, a German engineer engaged in trafficking in electronic material was arrested. It was possible to arrest him only by intercepting transmissions by fax and electronic mail. This was done for reasons that no one would have dared to contest, probably, since they are those of the secret services and drug squads operating between Hong Kong, Las Vegas, and New York. Apparently this German engineer was moreover a specialist on the subject of monitoring equipment intended, among other things, to interfere with the police's phone tappings. Subscribers to CompuServe received in their electronic mailboxes offers of equipment making it possible to intercept communications, to track them, to pick up conversations, and also to identify phone numbers. Another of these toys makes it possible to clone cellular phones by duplicating the features of a mobile. You then intercept the portable phone number and its serial number with a scanner (the one that was for sale in Germany), you get yourself to be taken for someone else, the subscriber gets the bills, and no trace of the parasite can be found. Let's say "parasite" because what this directs us to open up is indeed the general problematic of relationships between parasitism and hospitality. How can we distinguish between a guest and a parasite? In principle, the difference is straightforward, but for that you need a law; hospitality, reception, the welcome offered have to be submitted to a basic and limiting jurisdiction. Not all new arrivals are received as guests if they don't have the benefit of the right to hospitality or the right of asylum, etc. Without this right, a new arrival can only be introduced "in my home," in the host's "at home," as a parasite, a guest who is wrong, illegitimate, clandestine, liable to expulsion or arrest.

But current technological developments are restructuring space in such a way that what constitutes a space of controlled and circumscribed property is just what opens it to intrusion. That, once again, is not absolutely new: in order to constitute the space of a habitable house and a home, you also need an opening, a door and windows, you have to give up a passage to the outside world [*l'étranger*]. There is no house or interior without a door or windows. The monad of home has to be hospitable in order to be *ipse*, itself at home, habitable at-home in the relation of the self to itself. But what has always been structured like this is nowadays multiplying both the home and the accessibility of home in proportions and modalities that are absolutely unprecedented. Whence the profound homogeneity between the devices of the private, clandestine, non-state network, and those of the police network of state surveillance. Their shared technology makes it impossible for the two spaces and the two types of structure to be mutually impermeable.

Let's take another American example. There now exists something called a "lifetime phone," which saves 99 different combinations of two numbers in the memory of one phone. It is on the market ($1,900), sold by the company of this Bowitz person (the German engineer), but illegal and used by drug traffickers, kidnappers, etc. Well, a federal agent got himself introduced into the network and welcomed "with open arms" by getting himself taken for a trafficker in heroin. The German engineer had even suggested that he launder his heroin money in Hong Kong. The downfall of the mover of this high-tech machinery was his mail, which, for sales purposes, would arrive in practically anyone's electronic mailbox, for instance that of an AT&T employee, himself a CompuServe subscriber, who, after various maneuvers on the part of a private detective to whom he had confided the affair, met Bowitz, saw all the equipment, and eventually alerted the narcotics police and the American secret services. The New York judge made use of the laws authorizing phone tapping for the purpose of intercepting e-mail messages. So the directors of CompuServe, this network medium that was not in itself dishonest, put themselves at the service of the police. The CompuServe spokesperson declares: "It's the first time we had been confronted with a situation of this type. Concerning criminal matters, and in the presence of legal documents, it was natural for us to offer our services." The same person also said: "Pseudonyms and numbers can safeguard anonymity, but, if need be, it is always possible for us to recover the personal details of a subscriber who commits a crime: we always have their credit card number and their address." The credit card, like the code number—that today is the ultimate identity card and one of the major resources of the police. *Mutatis mutandis*, it's a bit like the situation of a mailman or post office employee who, faced with something that either is or is presented to him as criminally suspect, would agree to open the mail, to give mail to the police; or else, to speak closer to hospitality, the situation (a classic and common one, too) of a hotel manager working with the police. (Let's leave to one side the problems—only analogous, and only analogous in relation to each other—of the confessor and the psychoanalyst.) This can happen in hotels but also in night shelters or hospitals. This absolute porosity, this limitless accessibility of technical devices meant for keeping secrets, for encoding and ensuring secrecy, is the law, the law of the law: the more you encode and record in figures, the more you produce of this operational iterability which makes accessible the secret to be protected. I can hide a letter only by separating myself from it and thus by yielding it to the outside, by exposing it to another, by archiving it, a document thereafter accessible in the space where it is deposited.

This is the paradoxical effect of what we are here calling the pervertibility, the perversion of this state violence or this right, that is always possible and in truth virtually inevitable, bound to happen: the effacement of the limit between private and public, the secret and the phenomenal, the home (which makes hospitality possible) and the violation or impossibility of home. This machine renders impossible the hospitality, the right to hospitality, that it ought to make possible (always according to the contradiction or aporia that we have been formalizing since the start of this seminar).

As to this paradox and this aporia of a right to hospitality, of an ethics of hospitality which is limited and contradictory *a priori*, let us again recall another minor but so major text of Kant's, not the one on the law of universal hospitality with which we

*ity. Yet this Law of hospitality must continue to be thought, as a magnetization which "puts to the question" the composure of the laws of hospitality.*

*To allow in this way for there to be open places that give room for the "purposelessness" of philosophical discourse is already a political gesture, symbolically preserving a space where the essential, too, might be said and might arise.*

*"The question that the foreigner will address to them to open this great debate, which will also be a great fight, is nothing less than that of the political, of*

opened these seminars, but the one on a "supposed right to lie out of humanity" (1797), which we had also analyzed before. The imperative to veracity would be absolutely unconditional. One should always speak the truth, whatever the consequences. For if one granted some right to lie, for the best reasons in the world, one would threaten the social bond itself, the universal possibility of a social contract or a sociality in general. This unconditionality, even before being due to some normative prescription (which it is as well, of course), could be shown to be deduced from a simple, very simple *analysis* of speech, of a rhetorical, constative, descriptive exploration of the address to another, of its normativity or its intrinsic performativity. Just as any utterance implies a performative promising to address itself to someone else as such ("I am speaking to you, and I promise you the truth"), just as any speech act promises the truth (even and especially if I am lying)—well, anyway, I can always lie, of course (and who could swear or prove that Kant himself never lied?), but that will signify quite simply that therefore I'm not speaking to someone else, end of story. And in doing this, I am not recognizing either the essence of speech as giving one's word, or the necessity of founding a social bond. Now what is Kant *doing*, in following this logic, where it can appear *indisputable* (indisputable as testimony, even if it were logically refutable and even if it shocks everyone's good sense as it worried Benjamin Constant; he asked if you should hand over a friend who is staying with you to assassins who are looking for him, a question to which Kant replies without hesitating: "Yes, one should never lie, even to assassins")? Two operations in one, whence the ambiguity. *On the one hand*, in one single gesture, Kant founds pure subjective morality, the duty to speak the truth to the other as an absolute duty of respect for the other and respect for the social bond; he bases this imperative on the freedom and the pure intentionality of the subject; he reminds us of its basis through an inflexible analysis of the structure of the speech act: he also secures social right as public right. But simultaneously, *on the other hand*, in laying out the basis of this right, and in recalling or analyzing its basis, he destroys, along with the right to lie, any right of keeping something to oneself, of dissimulating, of resisting the demand for truth, confessions, or public openness. Now this demand constitutes the essence not only of law and the police, but of the State itself. In other words, by refusing the basis of any right to lie, even for humane reasons, and so any right to dissimulate and keep something to oneself, Kant delegitimates, or at any rate makes secondary and subordinates, any right to the internal hearth, to the home, to the pure self abstracted from public, political, or state phenomenality. In the name of pure morality, from the point where it becomes law, he introduces the police everywhere, so much and so well that the absolutely internalized police has its eyes and its ears everywhere, its detectors *a priori* in our internal telephones, our e-mails, and the most secret faxes of our private lives, and even of our absolutely intimate relationships with ourselves. This figure of the State or police no longer even needs sophisticated techniques to intercept intimate, criminal, or pornographic conversations. By the same token, the thinker of the cosmopolitan right to universal hospitality, the author of *Perpetual Peace: A Philosophical Sketch* (1795), is also, without there being anything fortuitous in this, the one who destroys at its source the very possibility of what he posits and determines in this way. And that is due to the juridicality of his discourse, to the inscription in a law of this principle of hospitality whose infinite idea should resist the law itself—or at any rate go beyond it at the point where it governs it. And there is also nothing fortuitous, it seems to me, if in "On a supposed right to lie out of humanity," the privileged example (and one put forward by Benjamin Constant himself, initially, in the great tradition of biblical narratives that we previously reconstituted, of the story of Lot in particular) refers to a situation of *hospitality*: should I lie to murderers who come to ask me if the one they want to assassinate is in my house? Kant's response—and his way of arguing is laborious but also confident (we could come back to this in the discussion if you like)—is "yes," one should speak the truth, even in this case, and thus risk delivering the guest to death, rather than lie. It is better to break with the duty of hospitality rather than break with the absolute duty of veracity, fundamental to humanity and to human sociality in general.

Does this mean that the Kantian host therefore treats the one who is staying with him as a foreigner? Yes and no. He treats him as a human being, but he sets up his relationship to the one who is in his house as a matter of the law, in the same way as he also does the relationships linking him to murderers, the police, or judges. From the point of view of the

*the beginning, has been the only act by which one or a number of persons, by virtue of a power conferred on them by others to represent them, can hinder, accomplish, or suspend an economic process by referring it to other values which are not quantifiable ones. But hasn't the madness of political utopia done enough harm in the twentieth century for us to beware of it in future! In fact, by turning into ideology, utopia has acquired a language linking it to the implacable logic of economic "efficiency," which it claimed to be against. Utopias from Marxism to fascism that are inscribed in*

law, the guest, even when he is well received, is first of all a foreigner, he must remain a foreigner. Hospitality is due to the foreigner, certainly, but remains, like the law, conditional, and thus conditioned in its dependence on the unconditionality that is the basis of the law.

So the question returns. What is a foreigner? What would a foreign woman be?

It is not only the man or woman who keeps abroad, on the outside of society, the family, the city. It is not the other, the completely other who is relegated to an absolute outside, savage, barbaric, precultural, and prejuridical, outside and prior to the family, the community, the city, the nation, or the State. The relationship to the foreigner is regulated by law, by the becoming-law of justice. This step would take us back to Greece, close to Socrates and Oedipus, if it wasn't already too late.

*the reality of a place, a country, a power, collapse at the very point of their constitution, in nostalgia for a timeless fixity that would keep in its hands the means of its exercise. Beneath our very eyes, the political has disintegrated in the subtle coils of that new economic value, efficiency, with it wiping out traces and imprints.*

*Today, starting from that radical unfamiliarity of language and death in a foreign land as Derrida or Levinas reflects on them, should we not hear in political utopia a "placelessness" which opens the possibility of the human "city"? That this "utopia" can nowadays*

74

# Step of Hospitality / No Hospitality
*Pas d'hospitalité*
Fifth seminar (January 17, 1996)

*Jacques Derrida*

*Pas d'hospitalité*: no hospitality, step of hospitality.

We are going. We are moving around: from transgression to transgression but also from digression to digression. What does that mean, this *step too many*, and transgression, if, for the invited guest as much as for the visitor, the crossing of the threshold always remains a transgressive step? if it even has to remain so? And what is meant by this *step to one side*, digression? Where do these strange processes of hospitality lead? These interminable, uncrossable thresholds, and these aporias? It is as though we were going from one difficulty to another. Better or worse, and more seriously, from impossibility to impossibility. It is as though hospitality were the impossible: as though the law of hospitality defined this very impossibility, as if it were only possible to transgress it, as though *the* law of absolute, unconditional, hyperbolical hospitality, as though the categorical imperative of hospitality commanded that we transgress all the laws (in the plural) of hospital-

*only be audible because it breaks its way in from the other, from that unexpected and always disturbing guest, is one of the "spectres"—in Derrida's sense—of our* fin de siècle.

*If "making time" is equivalent in Hebrew to "inviting," what is this strange understanding of language which demonstrates that in order to produce time there have to be two of you, or rather there has to be some otherness, a breaking in on the original other? The future is given as being what comes to us from the other, from what is absolutely surprising. So then language*

76

ity, namely, the conditions, the norms, the rights and the duties that are imposed on hosts and hostesses, on the men or women who give a welcome as well as the men or women who receive it. And vice versa, it is as though the laws (plural) of hospitality, in marking limits, powers, rights, and duties, consisted in challenging and transgressing *the* law of hospitality, the one that would command that the "new arrival"[1] be offered an unconditional welcome.

Let us say yes *to who or what turns up*, before any determination, before any anticipation, before any *identification*, whether or not it has to do with a foreigner, an immigrant, an invited guest, or an unexpected visitor, whether or not the new arrival is the citizen of another country, a human, animal, or divine creature, a living or dead thing, male or female.

In other words, there would be an antinomy, an insoluble antinomy, a non-dialectizable antinomy between, on the one hand, *The* law of unlimited hospitality (to give the new arrival all of one's home and oneself, to give him or her one's own, our own, without asking a name, or compensation, or the fulfilment of even the smallest condition), and on the other hand, the law*s* (in the plural), those rights and duties that are always conditioned and conditional, as they are defined by the Greco-Roman tradition and even the Judeo-Christian one, by all of law and all philosophy of law up to Kant and Hegel in particular, across the family, civil society, and the State.

That is definitely where this aporia is, an antinomy. It is in fact about the law (*nomos*). This conflict does not oppose a law to a nature or an empirical fact. It marks the collision between two laws, at the frontier between two regimes of law, both of them

77

non-empirical. The antinomy of hospitality irrec-
oncilably opposes *The* law, in its universal singularity, to a plurality that is not only a dispersal (laws in
the plural), but a structured multiplicity, determined
by a process of division and differentiation: by a
number of laws that distribute their history and
their anthropological geography differently.

The tragedy, for it is a tragedy of destiny, is that
the two antagonistic terms of this antinomy are not
symmetrical. There is a strange hierarchy in this.
*The* law is above the laws. It is thus illegal, transgressive, outside the law, like a lawless law, *nomos
anomos*, law above the laws and law outside the law
(*anomos*, we remember, that's for instance how
Oedipus, the father-son, the son as father, father
and brother of his daughters, is characterized). But
even while keeping itself above the laws of hospitality, *the* unconditional law of hospitality needs the
laws, it *requires* them. This demand is constitutive.
It wouldn't be effectively unconditional, the law, if it
didn't *have to become* effective, concrete, determined,
if that were not its being as having-to-be. It would
risk being abstract, utopian, illusory, and so turning
over into its opposite. In order to be what it is, *the*
law thus needs the laws, which, however, deny it, or
at any rate threaten it, sometimes corrupt or pervert
it. And must always be able to do this.

For this pervertibility is essential, irreducible, necessary too. The perfectibility of laws is at this cost.
And therefore their historicity. And vice versa, conditional laws would cease to be laws of hospitality if
they were not guided, given inspiration, given aspi-
ration, required, even, by the law of unconditional
hospitality. These two regimes of law, of *the* law and

## Hyperboles

*To finish, I would like to try to throw light on Derrida's particular way of "taking to the limit" one or a number of concepts. In order to pick out these hyperboles, I will sometimes have to transcribe his speech almost word for word. I will take two examples that I will deliberately not borrow from the seminars given in this book, so as to keep back the "suspense" of the philosophical narrative for the reader. The first is about madness, the second about ghosts.*

the laws, are thus both contradictory, antinomic, *and* inseparable. They both imply and exclude each other, simultaneously. They incorporate one another at the moment of excluding one another, they are dissociated at the moment of enveloping one another, *at the moment* (simultaneity without simultaneity, instant of impossible synchrony, moment without moment) when, exhibiting themselves to each other, one to the others, the others to the other, they show they are both more and less hospitable, hospitable and inhospitable, hospitable *inasmuch as* inhospitable.

Because exclusion and inclusion are inseparable in the same moment, whenever you would like to say "at this very moment," there is antinomy. The law, in the absolute singular, contradicts laws in the plural, but on each occasion it is the law *within* the law, and on each occasion *outside the law* within the law. That's it, that so very singular thing that is called *the* laws of hospitality. Strange plural, plural grammar of *two plurals that are different at the same time.* One of these two plurals says the laws of hospitality, conditional laws, etc. The other plural says the antinomic addition, the one that adds conditional laws to the unique and singular and absolutely only great Law of hospitality, to *the* law of hospitality, to the categorical imperative of hospitality. In this second case, the plural is made up of One + a multiplicity, whereas in the first case, it was only multiplicity, distribution, differentiation. In one case, you have One + n; in the other, n + n + n, etc. (Let us note parenthetically that as a quasi-synonym for "unconditional," the Kantian expression of "categorical imperative" is not unproblematic; we will keep it with some reservations,

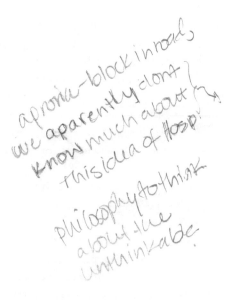

*aporia—block in road,*
*we aparently don't*
*know much about*
*this idea of Hosp.*

*philosophy to think*
*about the*
*unthinkable*

*Derrida begins by giving its due to the experiencing of "always" as fidelity in language to the other and to oneself. "Whatever the forms of exile," he says, "language is what one keeps for oneself."*

*He quotes Hannah Arendt who, when asked by a journalist, "Why have you remained faithful to the German language in spite of Nazism?" replied with these words: "What can one do, after all it's not the German language that went mad!" And she added: "Nothing can replace the mother tongue."*

*"As though Hannah Arendt could not imagine that*

under erasure, if you like, or under *epoche*. For to be what it "must" be, hospitality must not pay a debt, or be governed by a duty: it is gracious, and "must" not open itself to the guest [invited or visitor], either "conforming to duty" or even, to use the Kantian distinction again, "out of duty." This unconditional law of hospitality, if such a thing is thinkable, would then be a law without imperative, without order *Virtue* and without duty. A law without law, in short. For if I practice hospitality "*out of* duty" [and not only "*in conforming with* duty"], this hospitality of paying up is no longer an absolute hospitality, it is no longer graciously offered beyond debt and economy, offered to the other, a hospitality invented for the singularity of the new arrival, of the unexpected visitor.)[2]

To approach these antinomies, we had opened [Pierre Klossowski's] *Roberte ce soir* (1953) and begun to read the *inevitable* manuscript called *The Laws of Hospitality*, these "handwritten pages" that the uncle of the narrator, of the one who says "my Uncle Octave," had put above the bed, in the spare room, "on the wall of the bedroom kept for visitors"—and under glass. Inevitable but avoidable [*évitable*] manuscript, for where it is placed (above the bed and a bit separate, at the opening of the book), one ought to be unable not to make acquaintance with it, and yet one can always omit to read it.

He had had these "handwritten pages" "put under glass and framed in order to hang them on the wall of the bedroom kept for visitors." So here they are, hung up, high up: it is the place of law, this verticality of the on high, but also the site of what turns

*madness could inhabit language," Derrida remarks. Astonishment, or feigned surprise, which already brings about a first movement to the limit.*

*And he is indeed surprised that Arendt cannot imagine that language, the most intimate but also the most shared thing we have; that a language, insofar as it governs our relationship to the other and to the world, and whose law tears us away from a kind of silence, could be barbarism's accomplice. "As though the fragile edifice of Arendt's response wanted to preserve a possibility of redemption in the face of absolute evil,"*

up unexpectedly, inevitably, defying any horizon of expectation and any possible anticipation. Inevitable and inaccessible, intangible, these "handwritten pages" are placed above the bed, like the law, certainly, but as threatening as an epic above your head, in this place where the guest rests, but also where he won't have been able, where he wouldn't have been able, where he won't have had to fail to read the texts of a law of which no one is deemed ignorant.

Above their heads, whether the visitors are sleeping, dreaming, or making love, the laws keep watch. They watch over them, they oversee them from a place of impassivity, their glassy place, the tomb of this glass beneath which a past generation (here an uncle) must have laid them down, organized them, imposed them. A law is always laid down [*posée*], and even laid down against [*opposée à*] some nature; it is an instituted thesis (*nomos, thesis*). "Under glass," that's the laws of hospitality inaccessible to any transformation, intangible, presumably, but visible and more than visible, readable as the being of written laws must be. This is no longer the laws which, in what is supposed to be their own voice, speak to Socrates in the famous prosopopeia that we were listening to last time; these are written laws. They are only there, in short, to command—and to prescribe their own perversion. They are there, under glass, to watch over the guests and over their own perversion. They will wait for us while we make a long detour.

For these written laws immediately remind us of the ones that Antigone will have to transgress in order to offer her brothers the hospitality of the land and of burial: Antigone the foreign woman who ac-

*Derrida continues, guiding us toward what Arendt doesn't say. And he does this by pushing "the German language" toward the mother tongue and the adjective "mad" in the direction of complete madness, with its terrors and its blindnesses. He shows us that Arendt sows doubt where she would like to assure herself of certainty, in the way that denial shows up what it would like to eradicate the trace of. For Derrida's listening is quasi-psychoanalytic when he uncovers the dark side that supports the enigmatic place of the question.*

*Once this taking to the limit has been achieved,*

companies her father outside the law at the point where he is crossing a border and speaking to foreigners to ask them for hospitality; Antigone whose blind father, at the end of *Oedipus at Colonus*, again illustrates this strange experience of hospitality transgressed, through which you die abroad, and not always at all as you would have wanted.

We remember, from one digression to another: right at the start of the seminars, we had to displace the question of the foreigner. From birth to death. Usually, the foreigner, the foreign citizen, the foreigner to the family or the nation, is defined on the basis of birth: whether citizenship is given or refused on the basis of territorial law or the law of blood relationship, the foreigner is a foreigner by birth, is a born foreigner. Here, rather, it is the experience of death and mourning, it is first of all the law of burial that becomes—let us say the word—determining. The question of the foreigner concerns what happens at death and when the traveler is laid to rest in a foreign land.

"Displaced persons," exiles, those who are deported, expelled, rootless, nomads, all share two sources of sighs, two nostalgias: their dead ones and their language. *On the one hand*, they would like to return, at least on a pilgrimage, to the places where their buried dead have their last resting place (the last resting place of family here situates the *ethos*, the key habitation for defining home, the city or country where relatives, father, mother, grandparents are at rest in a rest that is the place of immobility from which to measure all the journeys and all the distancings). *On the other hand*, exiles, the deported, the expelled, the rootless, the stateless, lawless no-

mads, absolute foreigners, often continue to recognize the language, what is called the mother tongue,
as their ultimate homeland, and even their last resting place. That was Hannah Arendt's response on
one occasion: she no longer felt German except in
language,[3] as though the language were a *remains* of
belonging, although in fact, and we'll come to this,
things are more twisted. If it seems to be both, and
by that very fact, the first and the last condition of
belonging, language is also the experience of expro-
priation, of an irreducible *exappropriation*. What is
called the "mother" tongue is already "the other's
language." If we are saying here that language is the
native land, namely, what exiles, foreigners, all the
wandering Jews in the world, carry away on the soles
of their shoes, it is not to evoke a monstrous body,
an impossible body, a body whose mouth and
tongue would drag the feet along, and even drag
about under the feet. It is because this is about the
*step*, once again, of progression, aggression, transgression, digression. What in fact does language
name, the so-called mother tongue, the language
you carry with you, the one that also carries us from
birth to death? Doesn't it figure the home that never
leaves us? The proper or property, at least the *fantasy*
of property that, as close as could be to our bodies,
and we always come back there, would give place to
the most inalienable place, to a sort of mobile habitat, a garment or a tent? Wouldn't this mother
tongue be a sort of second skin you wear on yourself,
a mobile home? But also an immobile home since it
moves about with us?

Last time, we brought up those new teletechnologies, the telephone, the television, the fax or

*replaceable," harbors within it unreason, trauma, ha-
tred. It is in the image of the "unique and matchless
mother," Derrida insists, that mother in whom the
close, desiring, loving world can be changed into terror;
a mother who will be able to be given up without a
pause to madness. Out of what is most familiar arises
the anxiety that a senseless universe is being substituted
for the world given by the mother, in a way that is shat-
tering and almost unthinkable.*

e-mail, the Internet as well, all those machines that introduce ubiquitous disruption, and the rootlessness of place, the dis-location of the house, the infraction into the home. Well, speech, the mother tongue, isn't only the home that resists, the ipseity of the self set up as a force of resistance, as a counterforce against these dis-locations. Language resists all mobilities *because* it moves about with me. It is the least immovable thing, the most mobile of personal bodies, which remains the stable but portable condition of all mobilities: in order to use the fax or the "cellular" phone, I have to be carrying on me, with me, in me, as me, the most mobile of telephones, called a language, a mouth, and an ear, which make it possible to hear yourself-speaking.

What we are describing here, which is not the same as endorsing it, is the most unbreakable of fantasies. For that which doesn't leave me in this way, language, is also, *in reality*, *in necessity*, beyond the fantasy, that which never ceases to depart from me. Language only works *from* me. It is also what I part from, parry, and separate myself from. What is separated from me in parting from me. Hearing-yourself-speaking, this "auto-affection" of hearing-yourself-speaking-yourself, hearing-ourselves-speaking to each other, hearing-ourselves-speaking in the language or by word of mouth, that is the most mobile of mobiles, because the most immobile, the zero-point of all mobile telephones, the absolute ground of all displacements; and it is why we think we are carrying it away, as we say, with each step, on the soles of our shoes. But always while being separated from oneself like this, while never being quits with

*"The essence of madness must be related to the essence of hospitality, in the area of this uncontrollable outburst toward the one who is closest."*

Then Derrida brings about a new taking to the limit when he says of maternal madness that it gets us to glimpse something of the essence of madness. *He leads us to think of the mother tongue as a metaphor for "being-at-home in the other"—a place without place opening onto hospitality—and which as such gestures toward the* essence of hospitality.

These movements to the limit make readable for us the contamination of hospitality into an "uncontrol-

that which, leaving oneself, by the same step never stops quitting its place of origin.

What happens at the end of *Oedipus at Colonus*? As we were saying, Oedipus illustrates this strange law of hospitality: you die abroad and not always at all as you would have wanted it. In this tragedy of written and unwritten laws, before living the experience of the last duty to render one of her dead brothers, Antigone endures and names that dreadful thing: being deprived of her father's tomb, deprived above all, like her sister Ismene, of the *knowledge* as to the father's last resting place. And worse, in being deprived of this *by* the father, according to the wishes of the father himself. According to an oath. For at the moment of dying, Oedipus enjoins Theseus never to reveal to anyone, particularly his daughters, the whereabouts of his tomb. It is as if he wanted to depart without leaving so much as an address for the mourning of the women who love him. He acts as if he wanted to make their mourning infinitely worse, to weigh it down, even, with the mourning they can no longer do. He is going to deprive them of their mourning, thereby obliging them to go through their mourning of mourning. Do we know of a more generous and poisoned form of the gift? Oedipus doesn't even give his daughters the time of mourning, he refuses them that; but in doing so he also offers them, simultaneously, a limitless respite, a sort of infinite time.

[Counterpoint: secondary motive, relatively independent and superimposed polyphonically. From now on, what will be said of the death and burial of

*lable outburst toward the one who is closest," when the eruption of a violence that borrows its madness from the maternal is substituted for proximity. Derrida perceives the resurgence of an "intimate" violence of the same kind in events like hostage wars or terrorist acts against civilians, but the equally close thing that he interrogates, in this connection, is hospitality turning back into hostility, starting from the always possible perversion of the Law.*

*"The madness of the mother tongue," he says, "puts us on the track of a mother who lays down the law from*

Oedipus, of the father-son transgressor, of the father-son, of the father-brother-of-his-daughters outside the law (*anomos*), you can also hear as the counterpoint of a meditation that is almost silent, reticent, in the sense that *reticence*, as you know, is the figure of a deliberate *keeping-quiet* so that more than eloquence can be heard in it. It would be a matter of meditating, and so as to analyze it too, what has just happened between the cathedral of Notre-Dame in Paris and Jarnac: both the opposite of and the same thing as the burial of Oedipus, but also a one-off in the history of humanity, at any rate in the history of the State as such, in its statutory mode. Between two internments, one and two families, from one internment to the other: a single *paterfamilias*, a single master of the house and chief of State, private man and monarch, two sons and a single daughter, Antigone without Ismene, a single daughter who must keep a singular relationship to unwritten law. We won't say anything about it here, perhaps you will think about it yourselves at each step and we'll come back to it with no constraints, if you like, in the discussion time. There would be too much to say there for me to be able to make notes for a seminar.]

On the threshold of death, then, Oedipus declares to Theseus:

Son of Egeus, I am going to teach you [so it is a lesson, *didaxo*] what things are laid up for you and this city, unimpaired by age. I am going to lead you myself right now, without a guide to hold on to, to the place [*chōron*, like *chōra*, is the place, the interval, the placement, the stopping point, the land, the country] where I must die. (1518–22)

*the place of an outlaw." A maternal authority that Derrida relates to Oedipus, "who, from a place of burial kept secret from his daughters, intends to lay down the law with the secret entrusted to Theseus." "Perhaps then The law of pure hospitality as justice commands us to open up hospitality beyond the family?" he asks. But to reject the family (and any structure in which it is continued—civil society, the state, the nation) is to confirm pure hospitality in its impossibility. It must therefore be conceived of on the basis of this paradox.*

Oedipus thus thinks he will choose the dwelling place, his last dwelling place. He wants to be alone in doing it, he is the only one *to* decide it, the only one *for* that, alone *as* someone who signs, alone *because* he decrees such a choice and wants to get himself, by himself, to the place of his death and his burial. He conducts his own funeral in secret. Almost in secret, let us clarify, for *in asking for* a secret of this kind, he also has to confide it. He gets Theseus to swear secrecy.

It is true that he doesn't even reveal this secret *beforehand* to Theseus. He announces it, he lets it be known that there is a secret being kept, a secret to be kept, but he will reveal it only when they get there, beside the tomb, at the place of the last dwelling.

But don't tell anyone else, don't reveal either where it is hidden or the area it is in, so that it may always afford you strength of many shields or spears brought in from outside. But the things which are sacred and not moved by speech [literally: the most impure things, the most cursed, which must not be spoken, the secret that must not be violated by speech, the accursed thing that must not be touched, or set in motion by *logos*, by discourse, *a d'exagista mede kineitai logō*], you will learn yourself when you go there alone; as I would not reveal it to anyone. . . . [It is thus a cursed secret, this place where he will be dead and buried, and this secret he confides to someone, to Theseus, while telling him that he cannot even tell him it himself, to him in person. A bit as though he didn't know it, this secret that he tells Theseus he will find out for himself, and will thenceforth have to keep hidden, by accompanying him right to his last dwelling place, his last stay, his last habitat] . . . not to any of the townspeople or even to my own children, much as I love them ["*much as I love them*": as though loving were finally just what had

*"In Europe," he concludes, "this would be the space of all the battles to be fought."*

*In this final taking to the limit, Derrida lays out for us not only the problematic of The law and its per-vertibility, but also what is engendered in thought by the relationship to language inasmuch as it describes a universal structure. Invoking the writers and thinkers for whom "language was an acquired, not a maternal acquisition," Derrida cites this very fine sentence of Levinas: "The essence of language is friendship and hospitality." And he adds: "Against the sacredness of*

to be conveyed in this ultimate proof of love that consists in letting loved ones know *where* one dies, where one is *dead*, where one *is*: dead, *where* one is *once* dead, and as though Oedipus were deprived of the right of giving that ultimate proof of love to those to whom he vows his love and whom he loves, his daughters and his sons, here his daughters, Antigone and Ismene; and deprived as he is of revealing to the ones he loves the place of his death, *where he is dead*, where he is, dead, once dead, dead once dead, dead only once once dead once and for all, it is thus as though he were deprived of the daughters he has, as though he had no daughters, as though he no longer had any or had never had any] for I would not reveal it to anyone, not to any of the townspeople or even to my own children, much as I love them. But you keep it always [you save it always, *all'autos aiei sōze*, and the always, *aiei*, the "all (the) time," is the time of this greeting, of this saved secret as to the place where one is-dead], you keep it always and, when you come to the end of your life [*telos tou zèn*], tell it only to the most worthy, so that he in his turn, and so forth, may reveal it to his successor. . . .

In following the logic of this speech, in step with what we have just heard and what will follow, we see the extent of this calculation. And particularly of the conditions laid down. Tradition will be guaranteed at this price: good tradition, the one that will rescue the city, the one that will guarantee the political safety of the city, it is said that it will be borne, like tradition itself, through the transmission of a secret. Not just any living secret, but a secret concerning the clandestine site of a death, namely, the death of Oedipus. Secret knowledge, secret about knowledge, secret about knowing, ultimately, where dies the great transgressor, the outlaw, the blind *anomos* who cannot even himself confide the secret that he enjoins upon others to keep about the place where he, the foreigner, will be able once upon a time to have-died:

. . . tell it only to the most worthy, so that he in his turn, and so forth, may reveal it to his successor. In this way you will keep your city safe from the ravages of the men sprung from the sowing [the men sprung from the sowing is the race of Thebes, descended from the Dragon's teeth, sown by Cadmus. Thebes is daughter of the Earth]. So many cities [so many States], even if they are well governed, get excessively insolent [*hubris, kathubrizan*]! The eyes of the gods do perceive [the eyes of the gods are on the watch, like the laws above our heads—or above the bed or above death], and even belatedly, anyone who, having let go of religion, turns to madness [*mainesthai*]. Don't you, son of Aegeus, let that happen to you [fear of the coming war between Athens and Thebes]. (1530–38)

Oedipus then pushes on toward this place that he keeps secret. He wants to avoid being late for this sort of rendezvous with the gods. It would be worth following the motif of *delay* and haste, the time and the rhythm of this journey, the *halting* and *hastening* that mark the beat of this tragedy. Speaking to his daughters, Oedipus asks them to follow him. Up till then, it was they who were acting as guides to him, the blind one. From now on he will lead them. Blind as he is, it is he who is going, showing the way, it is he who is going to point out the path. He even asks them not to touch him. Here it is not the law that should remain untouchable, it's the *anomos*:

Come, and do not touch me, but let me find the sacred tomb [*ton ieron tumbon*] by myself, where it is fated for this man to be hidden in this earth [*kruphthenai chthoni*:

*you know that exiles, the deported, the expelled, no-*
*mads, and the uprooted, share two sources of grief and*
*nostalgia, their dead ones and their language. . . ."*
  *As strong as that is this expression of transhumant*
*death; what Derrida shows us to be the fragility of the*
*link that connects what is intimate and ephemeral in*
*subjectivity (the birth language) to what is most easily*
*read, manipulated, excavated, in burial (the corpse).*
*The dead one, who no longer belongs to us, who no*
*longer belongs to himself or to anyone but who was at*

that I be buried, concealed, dissimulated, that I disappear into my crypt]. (1544–46)

A foreigner in a foreign land, Oedipus thus takes himself toward a place of hiding [*clandestinité*]. A sort of illegal [*clandestin*] immigrant, he will be concealed there in death: buried, interred, carried in secret in the night of a crypt. He reverses the roles by himself, the blind one, leading his daughters and Theseus. But he is himself guided by Hermes and the goddess of the Underworld:

Yes, it is this way that I am led by the guiding Hermes and the goddess of the lower world. Lightless light [*O phōos aphegge*], before you were mine for a long time, and now for the last time my body feels you. (1547–50)

We listen to him, the blind man, the sightless foreigner, the foreigner outside the law who wants still to keep a right of regard over his last dwelling place. We hear him, this foreigner, this stranger, uttering his complaint strangely.

What is his grievance? What about his mourning? Why this final mourning? Like a dying person ritualistically saying farewell to the light of day (for if we are born seeing the day, we die ceasing to see the day), he weeps, he too, the blind one, deplores having soon to be deprived of the day. But here complaining of having to lose the light of a day that will never have been his own, the blind man weeps for a *tangible* light, a light caressed, a caressing sun. The day touched him, he was in contact with it, this light both tangible and touching. A warmth touched him invisibly. What he is going to be deprived of in secrecy, at the moment of this encrypting, of this encrypting of encrypting, at the moment when he is going to be hidden away buried in a hideaway, is the extraordinary contact of a light. There is a vocabulary dominating this last address that speaks of the semantic family of the crypt, the hiding place, secrecy. The address is cryptic, one could say, and if Oedipus gives it to his daughters and to Theseus, Theseus whom he calls "dearest of *xenoi*" (1552), he only addresses them with an abstract message: without knowing anything else, let them at least know that he is going to a secret place. He directs his steps toward a final dwelling place to pass away there, to be encrypted there, crypt in the crypt:

Now I am going to hide my last light in Hades. But dearest of hosts [one translation for dearest of strangers or foreigners, *philtate xenōn*, and the foreigners are hosts, Oedipus speaks to his host as to a foreigner at the moment when he is going to die in a foreign land but in a secret place], to this country, to all those who follow you, may you be happy, and in your good fortune remember me in my death, forever blessed. (1552–55)

It is the moment for him to pass away and encrypt himself, to let himself be encrypted at least twice, as though there were two places, two events, two moments of taking-place. Two times for the burial and the passing away of a body twice stolen, once in dying, in losing a light that he had already lost, in seeing himself deprived of a daylight of which he was *already* deprived, another time for being buried in a foreign land, and not only far away but at an inaccessible site. Oedipus then asks that he not be forgotten. He begs: to be kept dead. He requests it, he begs it, but this plea is an injunction, it raises the suspicion of a threat, it prepares the way for or announces a piece of blackmail. At any rate, it looks uncannily like it. Oedipus demands that he not be forgotten. Because look out! If he were forgotten everything would go badly! Now he addresses this threatening plea and this calculated injunction to the *xenos*, the dearest foreigner or host, the host as friend but a host who is friend and ally who thereby becomes a sort of hostage, the hostage of a dead man, the possible prisoner of a potential absent person.

The host thus becomes a retained hostage, a detained addressee, responsible for and victim of the gift that Oedipus, a bit like Christ, makes of his dying person or his dwelling-demanding, his dwelling-dying: this is my body, keep it in memory of me. The favorite foreigner or host, the well-loved Theseus to whom Oedipus speaks in this way (*philtate xenōn*) at the moment of his last willing, at the instant when he is confiding to him this equivocal housing of himself, the confided confidence of the secret of his crypt, the host chosen in this way is a hostage bound by an oath. He does not see himself as tied by an oath he would have spontaneously proffered, but by an oath (*orkos*) to which he has found himself—yes, *found*—unsymmetrically committed. Committed before the god, assigned by Oedipus's mere word. For the god watches over, he has kept his eye on the burial of this outlaw. And when Oedipus's daughters ask him if they can see the holy tomb (*ieron tumbon*), when they entreat him to let them accede to the secret place of the secret, Theseus will refuse, invoking the oath (*orkos*) that links him to the god. Everyone is hostage to the dead man, beginning with the favorite host, linked by the secret he has been given, confided, given to keep, that he must keep, obliged as a result by the law that falls upon him before he even has to choose to obey it.

(That puts us back on the track of the invisible theater of hospitality, the law without law of hostility, and even the war of the hostages. Let us recall Levinas's formulations, which we shall come back to in another register: "The subject is a host";[4] then, some years later, "The subject is hostage."[5])

The end of Oedipus. You hear a chorus's prayer: that the foreigner (*xenos*), Oedipus, should descend into the plain of the dead where everything is buried, in the house of the Styx. You hear two daughters who, after Theseus has committed himself on oath to respecting the secret, have to separate from their dying father, a father who then dies without too much delay. The theme of delay is insistent, as I was suggesting just now, throughout this scene. Perhaps it even harbors the theme of an organizing *contretemps*, the true master of the house throughout this scene of final hospitality. You mustn't be late, you must always reduce the lateness, you must always make a little more haste. You are always in some way late, the consciousness only anticipates, ever, one delay too many. The two daughters lament but they do not bemoan only the fact of never more seeing their father ("a night of death fell upon our eyes," says Antigone). They complain for themselves, but above all they complain *about* two things, they plead two causes and twice accuse: *on the one hand*, that their father died in a foreign land, that he should first of all have *wanted* to die far away, but *on the other hand*, hidden in the secret of a foreign land, that his corpse, *their* paternal corpse, should also be buried without a tomb. Not at all, perhaps, without a grave, but without a tomb, without a determinable place, without monument, without a localizable and circumscribed place of mourning, without a stopping point [*arrêt*]. Without a fixed [*arrêté*] place, without a determinable *topos*, mourning is not allowed. Or, what comes down to the same thing, it is promised without taking place, a determinable place, so thenceforth promised as an interminable mourning, an infinite mourning defying all work, beyond any possible work of mourning. The only possible mourning is the impossible mourning.

Complaints: while recognizing that her father's body, hidden away like this, is protected from seizure and reappropriation, Antigone thus complains. She complains *herself* and she complains *about* the other, against the other (*Klagen/Anklagen*). She complains that her father has died in a foreign land and moreover is buried in a place foreign to any possible localization. She complains of the mourning not allowed, at any rate of a mourning without tears, a mourning deprived of weeping. She weeps at not weeping, she weeps a mourning dedicated to saving tears. For she does, in fact, weep, but what she weeps for is less her father, perhaps, than her mourning, the mourning she has been deprived of, if we can put it like that. She weeps at being deprived of a normal mourning. She weeps for her mourning, if that is possible. *eyes for crying not seeing*

How can a mourning be wept for? How can one weep at not being able to go through one's mourning? How can one go through the mourning of mourning? But how can one do otherwise, when the mourning has to be finished? And the mourning of mourning has to be infinite? Impossible in its very possibility?

That is the question that is being wept through the tears of Antigone. It is more than a question, for a question doesn't cry, but it is perhaps the origin of all questions. And it is the question of the foreigner—of the foreign woman. These tears, who has ever seen them?

We are going to hear. These tears Antigone weeps, she weeps for the death of her father in a foreign land, and in a foreign land where, moreover, he has to remain hidden in his death, thereby becoming an even more foreign foreigner. What this death is, is the becoming-foreign of the foreigner, the absolute of his becoming-foreign. For in death, the visibility of the tomb would have been able to reappropriate the foreigner, it would have been able to signify a sort of repatriation for him. No, here, the dead one remains all the more foreign in a foreign land in that there is no *manifest* grave, no visible and phenomenal tomb, only a secret burial, an ungrave invisible even to his family, even to his daughter. She is presumably weeping, as we have just heard, for an impossible mourning. But she dares to direct it toward the dead man himself. For she apostrophizes him, cries out for him, challenges him. She still speaks, beyond death, to her father, to the spectre of her father the foreigner who is becoming foreign to her, now that she cannot even any longer go through her mourning of him (so it is definitely the question of the foreigner, in all senses, and the question of the woman foreign to the foreign man). Addressing petition and question to the foreign father,

outside the law, blind and dead, she asks him—first
of all and simply—to see her. Or rather, she asks him
to see her weeping, to see her tears. The tears say
that the eyes are not made primarily for seeing but
for crying. Let us listen to her, this Antigone, the
foreign weeping woman addressing the ghost of a father more than once outside the law, foreigner in
more than one way, foreigner for having come to die
in a foreign land, foreigner for being buried in a secret place, foreigner for being buried without a visible grave, foreigner in that he cannot be mourned
as should happen, normally, by his relatives in
mourning.

In complaining, and in complaining about her father's fate, as she is complaining, she says a terrifying thing, does Antigone. She dares to declare that
this awful fate, her father's destiny, he desired it.
This was the desire of Oedipus, the law of the desire
of Oedipus. Of this desiring body, desiring against
his will [*à son corps défendant*] but still desiring, of
this body carried off into death, of this Oedipus
who continues to desire from the bottom of the desire of this so very secret death, overencrypted and
without mourning, of this outlaw who lays down
the law from beyond his corpse, of this outlaw who
still claims to lay down the law in the foreign State
that buries him clandestinely, of this blind and dead
father, this father deceased, separated, who has de-
parted from her and whose face represents this law
of the law outside the law, of her one and only father, Antigone asks something clear: that he see her
at last, her, at this very moment, and see her weep.
More specifically: she commands him to *see* her
tears. The invisibility, the placelessness, the illocality

of an "of no fixed address" for death, everything that
removes her father's body from phenomenal exteriority: that is what is being wept for without being
seen by the eyes. This interiority of the heart, this invisible speech, that is what comes to the tears, what
comes to the eyes as tears, here is a suffering both intimate and infinite, the nocturnal secret that
Antigone asks her father to *see*. She asks him to see,
and to see the invisible, in other words to do the impossible, what is twice the impossible:

ANTIGONE: Yes, there can be a regret even for troubles.
For what was never dear was dear, when I did still hold
him in my arms. Oh father, oh dear one, oh you who
have put on the eternal darkness below the earth, not
even there shall you find yourself unloved by me or
her.

CHORUS: He did . . .

ANTIGONE: He did what he wished to do.

CHORUS: What was that?

ANTIGONE: He died in a foreign land as he desired to. He
has a bed deep down, well in the dark, forever, and he has
not left behind a grief that is unwept. For this eye of
mine mourns you with its tears, and I don't know how,
poor me, I can do away with such great suffering over
you. Alas, you desired to die in a foreign land, but you
died bereft of me in this way. (1697–1715)

Faced with this double impossibility, of letting a
blind and dead father see, and see her tears, there remains but one route for Antigone, suicide. But she
still wants to kill herself in this place where her father
is buried, in a place that is undiscoverable, and undiscoverable precisely because of the Oath of which

*is not a question here of going back over the trauma of the war, but of understanding why this radical disenchantment it produced affected something in our humanity, in that which "promises" us to another, and perhaps permanently. Is it not the first time in the west that the word, in what it opens up of the very possibility of the dimension of the promise and the oath, has been mutilated in this way? With Nazism, it was a whole people, nations, and thousands of individuals who saw themselves "bewitched" by a word whose pur-*

Theseus reminds her. For this illocality doesn't derive from some topological operation; it is decreed by a sworn pledge, by the Oath (Orkos) demanded—in fact, imposed, assigned—by Oedipus himself. Heteronomy, desire and law of the other, where the latter, the other, yes the latter, Oedipus the first man (Hegel), like Oedipus the last man (Nietzsche), wanted not only to pass away, but to become un-findable for his relations, removed from their mourning, carrying himself away and carrying them into the abyss of a mourning actually mourning its own mourning:

ANTIGONE: Let us hasten back there, my dear.

ISMENE: To do what?

ANTIGONE: A desire possesses me. . . .

ISMENE: What?

ANTIGONE: To see the underground home.

ISMENE: Whose?

ANTIGONE: Our father's, wretched as I am.

ISMENE: But how can that be right for us? Don't you see? . . . He died unburied, apart from all.

ANTIGONE: Take me there and then kill me. (1724–33)

It is then, at the moment of this Wish, that Theseus, who comes back, reminds them about the Oath. He reminds them of this son of Zeus who bears the (name of) Oath (Orkos). In order to re-main faithful to a sworn pledge, to avoid perjuring themselves, they must not see, see with their own eyes, the holy and last dwelling place of their father:

*pose was to denature words themselves. These words could no longer be pronounced by the deported, they were persuaded to give them up themselves in advance, since they no longer had anything human. Now speech is the only human quality that cannot be forced by anything other than itself—we commit perjury in words—and it is from the very inside of language that it has been forced, from a rationalization elevated to the height of an unimaginable perversion. No form of barbarism, no eruption of violence, no terrorist act,*

THESEUS: What is it you want me to agree to?

ANTIGONE: We wish to see our father's tomb ourselves.

THESEUS: But it is not permitted to go there.

ANTIGONE: What do you mean, lord, ruler of Athens?

THESEUS: Children, that man forbade me to allow anyone to approach the region or to address the holy spot he occupies. And he said that if I do this my country will be always free from grief. So the god heard this being said by us and so did Oath [Orkos], son of Zeus, who hears everything.

ANTIGONE: If that is what he wants, that is enough. But send us to ancient Thebes, in the hope that we may prevent the slaughter that is coming to our brothers. (1755–72)

This long digression via Oedipus at Colonus, between Paris and Jarnac, was in a way dictated to us, as a first approach, by a charter entitled "The Laws of Hospitality," a constitution inscribed on glass, and so untouchable and readable, above a bed. A bed of daydreaming and lovemaking, dreams or fantasies, life and death: "just above the bed." The charter had been put in this place by the head of the household, by a "master of the house" who, if the narrator is to be believed, had no "more urgent concern than that of letting his joy shine out upon anyone who, of an evening, might come to eat at his table and rest under his roof from the fatigues of the road. . . ." (see p. 83, above).

The master of the house "waits anxiously on the threshold of his home" for the stranger he will see arising into view on the horizon as a liberator. And from the furthest distance that he sees him coming,

*however radical it might be, had systematized the radical lie at the very beginning of speech. I see in the phenomenal development of the image and the media the after-effect of a broken pact with speech.* Disbelief, *as the English say, bearing on the very roots of our relationship to language, and by the same token to the Other, this third party who up till now has been the guarantor of the promise borne to another, to one's neighbor, in the oath, in that repeated form of address that I pronounce and receive as subject.*

the master will hasten to call out to him: "Enter quickly, as I am afraid of my happiness."

"Enter quickly," quickly, in other words, without delay and without waiting. Desire is waiting for what does not wait. The guest must make haste. Desire measures time since its abolition in the stranger's entering movement: the stranger, here the awaited guest, is not only someone to whom you say "come," but "enter," enter without waiting, make a pause in our home without waiting, hurry up and come in, "come inside," "come within me," not only toward me, but within me: occupy me, take place in me, which means, by the same token, also take my place, don't content yourself with coming to meet me or "into my home." Crossing the threshold is entering and not only approaching or coming. Strange logic, but so enlightening for us, that of an impatient master awaiting his guest as a liberator, his emancipator. It is *as if* the stranger or foreigner held the keys. This is always the situation of the foreigner, in politics too, that of coming as a legislator to lay down the law and liberate the people or the nation by coming from outside, by entering into the nation or the house, into the home that lets him enter after having appealed to him. It's *as if* (and an *as if* always lays down the law here) the stranger—some Oedipus, in fact, in other words the one whose guarded secret about the place of death was going to save the city or promise it salvation through the contract we have just read—*as if*, then, the stranger could save the master and liberate the power of his host; it's *as if* the master, *qua* master, were prisoner of his place and his power, of his ipseity, of his subjectivity (his subjectivity is hostage). So it is indeed the master, the one who invites, the inviting host, who becomes the hostage—and who really always has been. And the guest, the invited hostage, becomes the one who invites the one who invites, the master of the host. The guest becomes the host's host. The guest (*hôte*) becomes the host (*hôte*) of the host (*hôte*).

These substitutions make everyone into everyone else's hostage. Such are the laws of hospitality. They correspond to the advertised *Difficulties,* to the stated aporias, right from the opening lines of the book. They are initially reported, and by the narrator himself, in other words by the nephew, by someone from the family who is not the son in a direct line and who is going to behave as a quasi-parricide. These *Difficulties* will have been anticipated even before the quotation of the laws of hospitality "under glass." Can they be formalized? Yes, no doubt, and through a seemingly fairly simple antinomy. In other words, the simultaneity, the "at the same time" of two incompatible hypotheses: "One cannot at the same time take and not take, be there and not be there, enter when one is within."

Now the impossibility of that "at the same time" is at the same time what happens. Once and every time. It is what is going to happen, what always happens. One takes without taking. The guest takes and receives, but without taking them, both "his" guest and "his" wife, the narrator's aunt. We thus enter from the inside: the master of the house is at home, but nonetheless he comes to enter his home through the guest—who comes from outside. The master thus enters from the inside *as if* he came from the outside. He enters his home thanks to the visitor, by the grace of the visitor. While such an antinomy remains, as it has to, perfectly contradictory, the event, however, cannot last: "That only lasted an instant . . . ," the narrator clearly says, " . . . for in the end, one cannot both take and not take, be there and not be there, enter when one is within."

This duration without duration, this lapse, this seizure, this instant of an instant that is canceled out, this infinite speed contracted into a sort of absolute halt or haste—this is a necessity that cannot be outsmarted any more: it explains why one always feels late, and that therefore, at the same time, one always yields to precipitation, in the desire for hospitality or in desire *as* hospitality. At the heart of a hospitality that always leaves something to be desired.

So that we can comment on them later in the course of the discussion, let us just first emphasize the tenses of an improbable sequence, the temporal and antinomic modalities of these Laws, the impossible chronology of this hospitality, all that a discrete irony names *Difficulties*. What is difficult are the things that don't let themselves be *done* [*faire*], and that, when the limit of difficulty has been reached, exceed even the order of the possible, like *faire* (doing), *facture* (bill), *façon* (way, manner). What cannot be done here derives, it would seem, from time. These *Difficulties* always have the form of a becoming-time of time, and one could also take that for the incalculable timing of hospitality. Let us emphasize these temporal markers, the chonometry of this intrigue:

tion of nomadic peoples, and of all transhumance. Nomadic peoples, transhumant populations, are so now only as a result of war, when they are constrained and forced into exile. But that a family, an individual, a clan, should want, by itself, to change country, laws, and customs, is now—on the threshold of a Europe without frontiers—totally proscribed, for their history, their identity, their debts will pursue them and catch up with them as surely as if they were standing on a glass chessboard.

## Difficulties

When my uncle Octave took my aunt Roberte in his arms, it was wrong to think that he was the only one to take her. A guest was entering, although Roberte *completely in the presence* of my uncle, wasn't *expecting* him, and while she was afraid of the guest coming, because Roberte *was expecting* some guest with an irresistible resolution, *already* the guest *was looming up* behind her, although it was my uncle who was entering, *just in time* to *take by surprise* the fulfilled fright of my aunt, *taken by surprise* by the guest. But in my uncle's mind, *it only lasted an instant* and again my uncle was *on the point* of taking my aunt in his arms. *It only lasted an instant . . .* since in the end, one cannot both take and not take, be there and not be there, enter when one is within. My uncle Octave was asking too much if he wanted to *prolong the moment of the open door*, it was already a lot that he could have the guest appear at the door and that *at that very moment* the guest loomed up behind Roberte to enable Octave to feel he was himself the guest when, borrowing from the guest the gesture of opening the door, coming from the outside, he could from there perceive them with the feeling that it was he, Octave, who was *surprising* my aunt.

Nothing could give a better idea of my uncle's mentality than these handwritten pages that he had had put under glass and framed to hang from the wall of the bedroom reserved for visitors, just above the bed, with a few wild flowers wilting on the old-fashioned frame:

## The Laws of Hospitality

The master of the house having no *more urgent* concern than that of letting his joy shine out over anyone who, of an evening, will come to eat at his table and rest under his roof from the fatigues of the road, anxiously *awaits* on the threshold of his house the stranger he *will see* rising into view on the horizon like a liberator. And from as far away

*These different reflections raise the question of the necessity of exile in order for "oneself as another," in Paul Ricoeur's fine expression, to come into being. Only what does a way of thinking become when it is cut off from its roots from the outset, without there even having been the transmission of a meaning? And what do human beings become when dispossessed, not of their things nor even of their house, but of what links them to interiority? If burial is inseparable from language, as Derrida thinks, because we always take with us our*

as he sees him coming, the master will hasten to call out to him:

"Enter quickly, as I am afraid of my happiness."

Last time, in a slightly strange way, we displaced the question of the foreigner by inverting the order or the direction—really the very meaning—of the question. Letting ourselves be guided by outline rereadings of texts by Plato (*Crito*, the *Sophist*, the *Statesman*, the *Apology of Socrates*) or Sophocles (*Oedipus at Colonus*), we let ourselves be interrogated by certain figures of the foreigner. They reminded us of a previous one: before the question *of* the foreigner as a theme, the title of a problem, program of research, before assuming in this way that we already know *what* the foreigner *is*, what the foreigner *means*, and *who* the foreigner is, even before that, there was of course, again, the question *of* the foreigner as the question-demand addressed to the foreigner (who are you? where do you come from? what do you want? do you want to come? or what are you getting at? etc.); but above all, even earlier, the question *of* the foreigner as question *come from* abroad. And thus of response or responsibility. How should one respond *to* all these questions? How be responsible *for* them? How answer for oneself when faced with them? When faced with questions that are so many demands, and even prayers? In what language can the foreigner address his or her question? Receive ours? In what language can he or she be interrogated?

"Language"—let us understand this word in both a narrow sense and a broad sense. One of the numerous difficulties before us, as with settling the ex-

*words and our dead, what becomes of burials when they are moved nearer the hospital; when birth and death, secret and inalienable spaces of pain and of peace, are exiled away from "home"? These are some of the questions broached by these movements or passages.*

*These movements to the limit, or rather outside limits, hyperbolical as they are, teach us as much as thinking itself. They show us the shock of discovery. The written text undoes the breaks and dissonances of discourse, focusing on the continuous unwinding of its thread, but*

tension of the concept of hospitality or the concept of foreigner, is that of this difference but also this more or less strict adhesion, this stricture between what is called a broad sense and what is called a narrow sense. In the broad sense, the language in which the foreigner is addressed or in which he is heard, if he is, is the ensemble of culture, it is the values, the norms, the meanings that inhabit the language. Speaking the same language is not only a linguistic operation. It's a matter of *ethos* generally. A passing remark: without speaking the same national language, someone can be less "foreign" to me if he shares a culture with me, for instance, a way of life linked to a degree of wealth, etc., than some fellow citizen or compatriot who belongs to what used to be called (but this language shouldn't be abandoned too quickly, even if it does demand critical vigilance) another "social class." In some respects at least, I have more in common with a Palestinian bourgeois intellectual whose language I don't speak than with some French person who, for this or that reason, social, economic, or something else, will be more foreign to me in some kinds of connection. Conversely, if we take language in the strict sense, which doesn't include nationality, a bourgeois Israeli intellectual will be more foreign to me than a Swiss worker, a Belgian farm laborer, a boxer from Quebec, or a French detective. This question of language, in the sense we are calling narrow—namely, the discursive idiom that is not coextensive with citizenship (French and Québecois, or English and American people can basically speak the same language)—we would always find implicated, in endless ways, in the experience of hospitality. Inviting, receiving, asylum, lodging, go by way of the language or the address to the other. As Levinas says from another point of view, language *is* hospitality. Nevertheless, we have come to wonder whether absolute, hyperbolical, unconditional hospitality doesn't consist in suspending language, a particular determinate language, and even the address to the other. Shouldn't we also submit to a sort of holding back of the temptation to ask the other who he is, what her name is, where he comes from, etc.? Shouldn't we abstain from asking another these questions, which herald so many required conditions, and thus limits, to a hospitality thereby constrained and thereby confined into a law and a duty? And so into the economy of a circle? We will always be threatened by this dilemma between, on the one hand, unconditional hospitality that dispenses with law, duty, or even politics, and, on the other, hospitality circumscribed by law and duty. One of them can always corrupt the other, and this capacity for perversion remains irreducible. It *must* remain so. It is true that this abstention ("come, enter, stop at my place, I don't ask your name, nor even to be responsible, nor where you come from or where you are going") seems more worthy of the absolute hospitality that offers the gift without reservations; and some might also recognize there a possibility of language. Keeping silent is already a modality of possible speaking. We will have to negotiate constantly between these two extensions of the concept of hospitality as well as of language. We will also come back to the two regimes of a law of hospitality: the unconditional or hyperbolical on the one hand, and the conditional and juridico-political, even the ethical, on the other: ethics in fact straddling the two, depending on whether the living environment is governed wholly by fixed principles of respect and donation, or by exchange, proportion, a norm, etc. With regard to the two extensions of language, let me just rapidly set up *two* lines of research, two programs or two problematics. They are both restricted to language "in the narrow sense," to the natural or national language drawn on by discourse, utterance, elocution.

1. The auto-mobile of this "language we carry with us," as we were saying a little while ago, is not separate from all the technological prostheses whose refinements and complication are in principle unlimited (the mobile phone is only a figure for this), or, on the other side, if we can put it like that, from the aforementioned auto-affection of which the consensus is that it belongs, as its particular possibility, to the auto-mobility of the living thing in general. Is there hospitality without at least the fantasy of this auto-nomy? of this auto-mobile auto-affection of which language's hearing-oneself-speak is the privileged figure?

2. If the proper name does not belong to language, to the ordinary functioning of language, although that is dependent on it; if, as I tried to demonstrate elsewhere, a proper name cannot be translated like another word in the language ("Peter" is not the *translation* of "Pierre"), what consequences can we draw from this about hospitality? This assumes both the calling on and recalling of the proper name in its pure possibility (it's to you, yourself, that I say "come," "enter," "whoever you are and whatever your name, your language, your

sex, your species may be, be you human, animal, or divine. . . .").[6]

We are also tied down to the strangeness of the approach we are attempting by a sort of law. This law could also be described as a crossing of languages or codes. On one side, we pull things toward a general and abstract formalization, sometimes by interrogating "our" history, especially through literary or philosophical texts. On another side, some examples, among so many possible other ones, give us access to the field of urgent contemporary matters, both political and *more than* political (for this is precisely about the political and the juridical). But these urgent matters do not only bring the classical structures into the present. They interest us and we take a look at them at the points where they seem, as though of themselves, to deconstruct these inheritances or the prevailing interpretations of these inheritances. We tried to indicate this with the new teletechnologies and the way in which they affect the experience of place, territory, death, etc.

As to the hostage structure, it would also be necessary to analyze a sort of essential and quasi-ahistorical law or antinomy. We could do this starting from ancient examples or from Levinas's ethical statements, but also starting from that which transforms this problematic into new experiences, and even new hostage wars. What is going on in Chechnya, for instance, ought to be analyzed from this perspective at the point when the taking of hostages becomes a terrifying weapon in the course of a war we no longer know whether to call a civil war, or a war of partisans (in the sense that Carl Schmitt gives this expression), or a war that at different times sets fellow citizens against each other, those of the same religion, foreigners, etc. Hostages are no longer prisoners of war protected by the rights of wars or the rights of people. The taking of hostages has become classic in the singular conflicts that oppose fellow citizens who no longer want to be fellow citizens, and who thus aspire to becoming foreigners respected as the citizens of another country—but a country that is as yet nonexistent, a State to come. There are more and more of these restructurings of state-national boundaries, and not only in Europe. (Whatever the enigma of this name and the "thing" to which it refers, "Europe" perhaps designates the time and space propitious to this unique event: it was in Europe that the *law* of universal hospitality received its most radical and probably most formalized definition—for instance in Kant's text, *Perpetual Peace*, a constant point of reference for us and throughout the whole tradition that has carried it on.) Being European (former Yugoslavia) or para-European (Russia and the former USSR), these wars are perhaps not, literally or strictly speaking, colonial wars or wars of liberation led by colonized peoples, but they are often made to look like recolonization or decolonization movements.

If I had had the time, and if it were appropriate to give a slightly autobiographical note to my remarks, I would have liked to study the fairly recent history of Algeria from this point of view. Its impacts upon the present life of two countries, Algeria and France, are still acute, and in fact still to come. In what had been, under French law, not a protectorate but a group of French departments, the history of the foreigner, so to speak, the history of cit-

*questions held in forgetfulness or secrecy, as in this re-*
*mark: "If you don't do justice to hospitality toward an-*
*imals, you are also excluding gods."*

*This quasi-sibylline sentence of Derrida's not only*
*raises the immense problem of the relation between*
*the sacred and the profane, but also suggests that the*
*essences of animal and god perhaps have some un-*
*known correspondences. If we have effaced the traces of*
*totemic civilizations, should we not bring back from*
*this forgetting the place of a possible hospitality to ani-*
*mals, out of fear that the divine desert us in its turn?*

izenship, the future of borders separating complete citizens from second-zone or non-citizens, from 1830 until today, has a complexity, a mobility, an entanglement that are unparalleled, as far as I know, in the world and in the course of the history of humanity. I refer again to the article called "Le puzzle de la citoyenneté en Algérie" [The puzzle of citizenship in Algeria]" by Louis-Augustin Barrière, in the journal *Plein Droit*, issues 29–30 (November 1995). At the beginning of colonization and until the end of World War II, Algerian Muslims were what was called "French nationals" but not "French citizens," a subtle but decisive distinction. Basically, they did not have citizenship in the strict sense, without being absolute foreigners. At the time of the annexation of what are called at the time, in a ruling of July 1934, "French possessions in North Africa," the inhabitants of this country, the Muslims, Arabs, or Berbers, and the Jews, remain subject to a religious law. Thirty years later, in 1865, these natives legally gain the status of French person without French citizenship. They could thus apply for civil service posts, but their status was French person without French citizenship. Nevertheless, the texts allowed for the native who was French but not a citizen to be able to aim for citizenship if, under certain conditions, he abandoned his particular position and if the public authority, ultimate judge in the matter, agreed. Access to French citizenship was made faster for indigenous Jews by the famous Crémieux decree of October 24, 1870, which was then abolished by Vichy, without the slightest intervention or demand on the part of the Germans, who at the time occupied only a part of (European) France. It is always war that makes things change. After World War I (and so many Algerian deaths at the front), a law of February 1919 takes a further step, offering French citizenship to Algerian Muslims via a procedure that no longer involved the discretionary arbitration of the French State. But it was another failure, both because the administration did not encourage Muslims and because they resisted a citizenship whose price was in fact the abandonment of their personal status (meaning in particular religious law, etc.). In short, they were being offered the hospitality of French citizenship on condition that they give up— in a pattern that is by now familiar to us—what they thought of as their culture. Before World War II, another advance (the famous Blum-Violette proposition) guarantees citizenship without the abandonment of Muslim personal status to all persons presumed assimilated by reason of their military service status, or their academic, commercial, agricultural, administrative, or political qualifications. Another failure. After World War II, and again because of the participation of Algerian soldiers in the defense and liberation of France, a new advance: on March 7, 1944, a ruling grants both citizenship and equality between all French citizens of Algeria with no distinction of origin, race, language, and religion, with the rights and obligations allowed for by the preamble and Article 81 of the Constitution. And yet there is still a distinction between two colleges of electors—which was no doubt not foreign, at least as one of its causes, to the rebellion that led to Algerian independence. In the first college were non-Muslims and certain Muslims meeting particular conditions (school diplomas, etc., services rendered in the army, decorations, rank of officer—and not sub-officer, sub-officers among whom were many of the leaders of the rebellion in 1954). This double college lasted until the Algerian War. Since Algerian independence, these "complications" have continued right up to the moment of the so-called Pasqua laws and the "standardization" that now subjects Algerians to the same conditions as other foreigners for their coming to France (the Evian agreements had allowed for special arrangements that exempted Algerian citizens from needing visas for France: "The time of the Evian agreements has passed," a collaborator of M. Pasqua replied to us when we were protesting against the said standardization).

Before ending today, we will restrict ourselves to two looks ahead or two protocols.

First let us consider the distinction between unconditional hospitality and, on the other hand, the rights and duties that are the conditions of hospitality. Far from paralyzing this desire or destroying the requirements of hospitality, this distinction requires us to determine what could be called, in Kantian language (in an approximate and analogical way, since in the strict sense they are in fact excluded in this case, and this exclusion needs to be thought about), intermediate *schemas*. Between an unconditional law or an absolute desire for hospitality on the one hand and, on the other, a law, a politics, a conditional ethics, there is distinction, radical heterogeneity, but also indissociability. One calls forth, involves, or prescribes the other. In giving a right, if I can put it like that, to unconditional hospitality, how can one give *place* to a determined, limitable, and delimitable—in a word, to a calculable—right or law? How can one give place to a concrete politics and ethics, including a history, evolutions, actual revolutions, advances—in short, a perfectibility? A politics, an ethics, a law that thus answer to the new injunctions of unprecedented historical situations, that do indeed correspond to them, by changing the laws, by determining citizenship, democracy, international law, etc., in another way? So by really intervening in the condition of hospitality in the name of the unconditional, even if this pure unconditionality appears inaccessible, and inaccessible not only as a regulatory idea, an Idea in the Kantian sense and infinitely removed, always inadequately approached, but inaccessible for the structural reasons, "barred" by the internal contradictions we have analyzed?

The second look ahead will take the form of an epigraph and a reference. All the examples we have chosen up till now bring out the same *predominance* in the structure of the right to hospitality and of the relationship with the foreigner, be he or she guest or enemy. This is a conjugal model, paternal and phallogocentric. It's the familial despot, the father, the spouse, and the boss, the master of the house who lays down the laws of hospitality. He represents them and submits to them to submit the others to them in this violence of the power of hospitality, in this force of ipseity that we have been analyzing for several weeks. We had also recalled the fact, at one point, that the problem of hospitality was coextensive with the ethical problem. It is always about answering for a dwelling place, for one's identity, one's space, one's limits, for the *ethos* as abode, habitation, house, hearth, family, home. So we should now examine the situations where not only is hospitality coextensive with ethics itelf, but where it can seem that some people, as it has been said, place the law of hospitality above a "morality" or a certain "ethics."

In order to indicate the direction of this difficult question, we could bring up the well-known history of Lot and his daughters. It is not alien to the tradition of the example cited by Kant in "On a supposed right to lie out of humanity," after St. Augustine in his two great books on lying. Should one hand over one's guests to criminals, rapists, murderers? or lie to them so as to save the people one is putting up and for whom one feels responsible? In Genesis (19:1ff.), this is the moment when Lot seems to put the laws of hospitality above all, in particular the ethical obligations that link him to his relatives and family, first of all his daughters. The men of Sodom demand to see the guests whom Lot is putting up, those who came to his home that night. The men of Sodom want to see these guests in order to "penetrate" them, says one translation (Chouraqui's: "Get them to come out to us: let's penetrate them!"), to "get to know" them, another modestly puts it (Dhorme's in the Pléiade collection: "Get them to come out to us so that we can get to know them"). Lot is himself a foreigner (*gēr*) come to stay (*gūr*) with the Sodomites. In order to protect the guests he is putting up *at any price*, as family head and all-powerful father, he offers the men of Sodom his two virgin daughters. They have not yet been "penetrated" by men. This scene follows straight after the appearance of God and his three messengers to Abraham, who offers them hospitality, at the oaks of

Mamre. We will return there later, it is the great founding scene of Abrahamesque hospitality, the major point of reference for Massignon's *L'hospitalité sacrée* or *La parole donnée*:

> When the two angels reached Sodom in the evening, Lot was sitting at the gate. As soon as Lot saw them he rose to meet them and bowed to the ground. "I beg you, my lords," he said, "please come down to your servant's house to stay the night and wash your feet. Then in the morning you can continue your journey." "No," they replied, "we can spend the night in the open street." But he pressed them so much that they went home with him and entered his house. He prepared a meal for them, baking unleavened bread, and they ate.
>
> They had not gone to bed when the house was surrounded by the men of the town, the men of Sodom both young and old, all the people without exception. Calling to Lot they said, "Where are the men who came to you tonight? Send them out to us so that we may abuse them."
>
> Lot came out to them at the door, and having closed the door behind him said, "I beg you, my brothers, do no such wicked thing. Listen, I have two daughters who are virgins. I am ready to send them out to you, to treat as it pleases you. But as for the men, do nothing to them, for they have come under the shadow of my roof."[7]

Sodomy and sexual difference: the same law of hospitality gives rise to an analogous bargaining, a sort of hierarchy of the guests and the hostages, in the famous scene on Mount Ephraim in Judges. After having welcomed a pilgrim on a journey, with his entourage, near Beit Lehem, their host receives a visit from the Benéi Balia'a; who ask to "penetrate" ("in the sexual sense," the translator specifies) the pilgrim:

*that, in the fixity of our mourning, we have perhaps forgotten this movement of invitation which is hospitality, and sacrificed a little of our humanity to the desire to know.*

*I thank Jacques Derrida for having offered to what are sometimes the austere lands of philosophy the hospitality of a kind of speaking that does not fear to confront the ghosts and to open up paths across to the living.*

Then the master of the house went out to them and said, "No, my brothers; I implore you, do not commit this crime. This man has become my guest; do not commit such an infamy. Here is my daughter; she is a virgin; I will give her to you. Possess her, do what you please with her, but do not commit such an infamy against this man." The men would not listen to him. So the Levite took his concubine and brought her out to them. They had intercourse with her and outraged her all night till morning; when dawn was breaking they let her go.

At daybreak the girl came and fell on the threshold of her husband's host, and she stayed there till it was full day. In the morning her husband got up and opened the door of the house.[8]

The end of the story, its *envoi*, if we can call it that, is better known. In the name of hospitality, all the men are sent a woman, to be precise, a concubine. The guest, the "master" of the woman, "picked up his knife, took hold of his concubine, and limb by limb cut her into twelve pieces; then he sent her all through the land of Israel. He instructed his messengers as follows, 'This is what you are to say to all the Israelites, "Has any man seen such a thing from the day the Israelites came out of the land of Egypt, until this very day? Ponder on this, discuss it; then give your verdict." ' And all who saw it declared, 'Never has such a thing been done or been seen since the Israelites came out of the land of Egypt.' "[9]

Are we the heirs to this tradition of hospitality? Up to what point? Where should we place the invariant, if it is one, across this logic and these narratives?

They testify without end in our memory.

# Notes

INVITATION

1. An obsession already betrayed by many of the seminar themes by themselves: "Bearing Witness," "Friendship," "Secrecy," "Rhetoric of Cannibalism."

2. The Latin *hostis* means guest but also enemy.

3. Kierkegaard, "Concluding Unscientific Postscript" (1846), in Robert Brettall, ed., *A Kierkegaard Anthology* (New York: Modern Library, n.d.).

4. Friedrich Nietzsche, *Thus Spoke Zarathustra*, trans. Walter Kaufmann (New York: Modern Library, 1995), p. 320.

5. Friedrich Nietzsche, *Ecce Homo*, trans. Walter Kaufmann (New York: Vintage Books, 1969), p. 261.

6. J. Patočka, *Liberté et sacrifice: Ecrits politiques*, trans. E. Abrams (Grenoble: Jérôme Millon, 1990), p. 36.

7. With regard to Patočka's interpretation of Antigone, H. Déclève beautifully writes: "Man is not only schism, he is at the same time reconciliation. From direct contact with night, with what is frightening, with the dead, gushes forth the obscure clarity of a law and a meaning more suitable than those of the stubborn reason of man. That is what we are reminded of by the character of

Antigone, in its originary femininity" ("Le mythe de l'homme-dieu," in Marc Richir and Etienne Tassir, eds., *Jan Patočka: philosophie, phénoménologie, politique* (Grenoble: Jerôme Millon), p. 131.

8. J. Patočka, *Platon et l'Europe*, seminars of 1973, trans. E. Abrams (Paris: Lagrasse, Verdier, 1983), p. 52.

9. Patočka, *Platon*, p. 53.

10. Patočka, *Platon*, p. 59.

11. See Derrida, *The Gift of Death* (1992), trans. David Wills (Chicago: Chicago University Press, 1995).

12. Patočka, *Platon*, p. 141.

13. "Il court, il court, le furet"—"he's running, he's running, the ferret"—is the line repeated in a game resembling "Hunt the Slipper." Players sit in a circle and pass around the "ferret" while another player, in the middle, has to guess where it is.—Trans.

14. As Mme Maeght detested cats that ate birds, he gave her as a birthday present a bronze cat holding out a tray between its paws. "For the crumbs . . . ," said Giacometti with a smile.

## FOREIGNER QUESTION

1. Plato, *The Apology of Socrates*, 17c–d. (*Summary of an improvised development of this of which only an abridged note remains here*: What we must be attentive to here, so as to comment upon it and explicate it at length, is the socio-cultural difference between languages, codes, connotations, within the same national language, the languages in the language, the effects of "foreignness" in domesticity, the foreign in the same. A lot could be said about languages within a language: whence the cleavages, the tensions, the virtual or oblique conflicts, declared or deferred, etc.)

2. "L'hospitalité," in Emile Benveniste, *Le vocabulaire des institutions indo-européennes* (Paris: Minuit, 1969), p. 94.—Trans.

3. Plato, *Crito*, 50a–e.

4. Sophocles, *Oedipus at Colonus*, ll. 1–40.

5. Sophocles, *Oedipus at Colonus*, ll. 42, 87–90, 123–25, 142.

6. Sophocles, *Oedipus at Colonus*, ll. 510–48.

STEP OF HOSPITALITY / NO HOSPITALITY

1. *Arrivant* is italicized, hinting at the relationship of the arrival to the *revenant*, or "returner," meaning a ghost.—Trans.

2. On the logic of such a commitment, of a "duty" without debt or without duty, compare for instance [Derrida,] *Passions* (Paris: Galilée, 1993), pp. 88ff. It is thus not a matter here, or there, if one is willing to read, of repeating the Kantian argument about what is "conforming to duty" (*pflichtmässig*), but on the contrary, against and without Kant, of carrying oneself beyond debt and duty, and thus even beyond what is done out of sheer duty (*aus reiner Pflicht*). To be continued.

3. Derrida, *Monolingualism of the Other*, trans. Patrick Mensah (Stanford, CA: Stanford University Press, 1999), pp. 84ff.

4. Emmanuel Levinas, *Totality and Infinity: An Essay on Exteriority*, trans. Alphonso Lingis (Pittsburgh, PA: Duquesne University Press, 1969), p. 299.

5. Emmanuel Levinas, *Autrement qu'être ou au-delà de l'essence* (The Hague: Martinus Nijhoff, 1974), p. 142; cf. also pp. 150, 164, 179, 201, 212, and the whole chapter on "Substitution." My reading of Levinas has been elaborated since the time of this seminar: see Derrida, *Adieu to Emmanuel Levinas*, trans. Pascale-Anne Brault and Michael Naas (Stanford, CA: Stanford University Press, 1999).

6. These two points had been extensively developed in the course of an improvised discussion of which no trace was kept.

7. Genesis 19:1–9, *The Jerusalem Bible* (London: Darton, Longman, and Todd, 1966).

8. Judges 19:23–30.

9. As we know, Rousseau was invested in this episode,

interpreted it, transformed it. In the *Essai sur l'origine des langues* [Essay on the origin of languages] as well as in *Le Lévite d'Ephraïm* [The Levite of Ephraim] of which he says in the *Confessions* that "if it isn't my best work, [it] will always be my favorite." See the fine analysis of these texts offered by Peggy Kamuf in a complete chapter of *Signature Pieces: On the Institution of Authorship* (Ithaca, NY: Cornell University Press, 1988), pp. 79–100.

*Cultural Memory* | *in the Present*